LEGENDS

OF

DERBYSHIRE

by

JOHN N. MERRILL

Trail Crest Publications Ltd.,
- from footprint to finished book."

1992

TRAIL CREST
PUBLICATIONS
Ltd.,
WINSTER,
MATLOCK,
DERBYSHIRE.
DE4 2DQ
☎ **Winster (0629) 650454**
FAX Winster (0629) 650416

Concieved, edited, typeset, designed, paged, marketed and distributed by John N. Merrill.

© Text - John N. Merrill 1992.

First Published - 1972
Reprinted - 1975 & 1979.
This edition - August 1992.

ISBN 0 874754 00 4

U.S.A.
office -
P.O.Box 124.
Santa Rosa,
New Mexico.
88435
U.S.A.

Typeset in - Palatino - bold, italic and plain 10pt and 18pt.

Printed by - John N. Merrill at Milne House, Speedwell Mill, Miller's Green, Wirksworth, Derbyshire. DE4 4BL

Cover sketch © Trail Crest Publications Ltd. 1992.

An all British
product.

ABOUT THE AUTHOR -

Likes to walk and write books.....so far hiked more than 150,000 miles and written over 100 guide books!

"from footprint to finished book"

OTHER BOOKS by John N. Merrill Published by TRAIL CREST PUBLICATIONS Ltd.

☞ Full list from TRAIL CREST PUBLICATIONS Ltd., Winster, Matlock, Derbyshire. DE4 2DQ

Contents

INTRODUCTION

It still amazes me how many tales and legends there are in Derby shire. Whether you walk, cycle or drive in the county, you never know what happy or unpleasant events occurred just where you are passing. During my research for this book I have accumulated information and facts relating to over a hundred tales. In this book I have included only twenty-four, of all manner of events of murders, marriages, romances, battles, curious oddities and remarkable men. I hope I have maintained a balanced selection of stories of yesteryear.

The tales are grouped in geographical order, beginning at the northern end of the Peak District and progressing southwards. Several are interwoven, and these I have indicated. All the locations mentioned can be found on the Ordnance Survey Maps, the I " Tourist edition— "The Peak District"—containing the majority of them. Where the tale refers to a name on the map rather than to a village or town, I have given a grid reference. Where it is possible to see physical evidence of a tale, such as a gravestone, I have mentioned it.

I have been enthralled researching for these stories, and hope that after reading them you will derive more pleasure from your travels in Derbyshire and the Peak District.

John N. Merrill.
Derbyshire. 1992

LOVER'S LEAP'S OF DERBYSHIRE

There are three such "leaps" in Derbyshire at Buxton, Stoney Middleton and Dovedale. All three have tales which are supposed to be the reasons why they were so called. From the few scraps of information available, the following are the tales.

Buxton

A mile east of the centre, along the A6 road, Ashwood Dale narrows and on your right is a small hill known as Lover's Leap. (Grid Ref. 072727).

A young couple had fallen in love, much to the disapproval of their parents. As time passed by, both parents' attitudes became unbearable, and the only solution left was to run away. Their plan was to leave their respective homes in the middle of the night, mount a couple of horses and ride to Peak Forest to be married. On the chosen night they crept out, met and set off together. They had not gone far when they heard a party following. Immediately they recognised the pursuers as friends of their parents—their plan had been betrayed.

However, they were determined to get away, and therefore rode hard and furiously with the party close behind. Nearing the top of the hill the young lady's horse cast a shoe, but her lover picked her up and together they continued to the top. Ahead was a wide gap. Not having any alternative, the only way to happiness was to jump.

This they did, and when the pursuers arrived they stared unbelievably at the gap and the lovers on the other side. They could not or dare not make the jump, leaving the lovers to continue their journey.

There this delightful tale ends, leaving one curious as to how they fared through life. We can only surmise that they lived happily ever after!

Stoney Middleton

This tale is authentic, because a tombstone to Hannah Baddaley exists in the churchyard. Unfortunately, through the course of time, the lettering has become illegible. The cafe, known as Lover's Leap Cafe, lies at the base of the leap. (Grid Ref. 229756.)

In 1762, Hannah Baddaley was acknowledged as the most beautiful girl in Stoney Middleton. Many a man tried to win her but none had any success. One person who would not give up his attempt was William Barnsley. After sheer persistence she began to like William, and as time went by they became deeply in love. For almost a year one could see them walking in the neighbour hood like a couple of cupids.

Then for no apparent reason William began to lose interest, until he ceased to see her completely. Hannah was heartbroken and repeatedly went looking for him When he saw her he ran away, which made Hannah's burden worse. The only way to erase his memory and end her unhappy life was to jump off one of the precipices which adorned the sides of Middleton Dale. The decision made, the very next day she ascended a slope and stood on top of an eighty foot high cliff. Placing her bonnet and hand kerchief on the ground, she walked to the edge and said the following:

> *"Oh! my William! my William—false William—no, I will not call thee false! My love! My life! Never, never again will mine eyes behold thee! Thee whom I loved—ah! I love thee still! O my love, wilt thou not come to my grave, and shed one tear to the memory of her, who died for thee? I'll bless thee again, my love, and then from this dizzy height I'll cast myself and prove to thee and the world—my love is stronger than death! I sink! I go, my love, my love!"*

Then she jumped. She hit a rock and scratched herself against some thorns before she landed safely! Petticoats in those days were made of wool, and soon after she jumped her petticoat opened out and acted as a parachute. The villagers were soon on the scene and escorted her, although bruised and shaken, back home. The jump had done one good thing; she had forgotten about her love affair. Hannah is supposed to have lived happily, though unmarried, for a couple of years afterwards before dying on December 12th, 1764, at the age of 26.

The above is verified by several other accounts of the tale, but her death at an early age raises a query. One book carried the above version except for the ending, which was thus: "After she had jumped, her fall was broken by some trees, before she landed in a saw pit! Shortly afterwards, several of the villagers found her and carried her home. Here she began to recover from her injuries, but died two years later." This account would seem a more realistic one and would explain her early death.

Dovedale

Just north of Sharplow Point, in Dovedale, is another Lover's Leap, although it is often omitted from maps of the area. (Grid Ref. 146517). The spot is an excellent viewpoint for much of Dovedale and has a steep drop down to the river Dove.

The tale is another one of a broken love affair. Again the only way the lady could terminate her life was to jump off this point. She jumped, but because of the numerous bushes at the bottom her fall was broken and cushioned, leaving her able to get up and walk away! No more evidence is available and we can only conjecture that she lived happily, though singly, for a good num ber of years afterwards.

According to several old books by Derbyshire authors there is a Lover's Leap at Matlock. Despite exhaustive research I have not been able to discover what the story is. The nearest fact I have found is Lover's Walk at Matlock Bath which still exists today and is just as popular!

METHODS OF PUNISHMENT
IN DERBYSHIRE

DERBYSHIRE has witnessed many forms of punishment for a variety of crimes. Some were brutal while others were by comparison mild but effective. Several represented the last occasion when the sentence was performed in the county—the gibbet for example. All death sentences were witnessed publicly until 1868, when this practice was abolished.

Burnt to Death

This was a rare sentence, on average only carried out about once a year in the whole of the country, and was generally reserved for women heretics. However, two cases in Derbyshire were for murder. In 1601, Joan Waste, having poisoned her husband, was burnt to death in the Windmill Pit, Derby. A plaque recalling her death can be seen in the porch of Birchover church, which is situated just down the lane on the left of The Druid Inn. At the road junction is an unusual sign pointing the direction to the church and illustrating a group of men walking to it. The other instance, in 1693, was of a young girl for murdering her employer.

Pressed to Death

Originating in Henry the fourth's reign (1367-1413), this punish ment was exercised on people who refused to plead guilty or remained silent when asked questions. A woman was pressed to death in 1665 in Derby for acting in such a manner. If a person remained silent, the judge would warn the accused three times before he passed the "Judgment of Penance" as it was called. It ran something like this—

> "That you be taken back to the prison whence you came, to a low dungeon into which no light can enter, that you be laid on your back on the bare floor, with a cloth around your loins but elsewhere naked; that there be set upon your body a weight of iron as great as you can bear—and greater, that you have no sustenance, save on the first day, three morsels of the coarsest bread, on the second day three draughts of stagnant water from the pool nearest to the prison door, on the third, again three morsels of bread as before and such bread and such water alternately from day to day, until you die."

Hung, Drawn and Quartered

There are several instances in Derbyshire of this gruesome sentence. The last one was on May 1st, 1820, when five conspirators were hung and then beheaded. An early example was in 1588. Sentenced to death in this manner were Richard Sympson and two priests, one of whom was Nicholas Garlick who preached at Padley Chapel, near Grindleford. If you go inside this chapel a stained glass window depicts the execution.

Another case was for the three ringleaders of the Pentrich Rebellion, Jeremiah Brandreth, William Turner and Isaac Lud lam. Pentrich is just south of Ripley. The sentence was conferred in Derby in 1817 and the Prince Regent signed the execution's authorisation on November 1st, 1817, but ruled that the quarter ing should not take place. The High Sheriff, Mr. Thomas Hal lowes, planned with the prison surgeon to remove the heads with a knife. But after consultation with London they employed the local blacksmith, a Mr. Bamford, to make a couple of axes similar in design to those in the Tower of London. The blade was 8" wide and a foot long. The local joiner, a Mr. Finney, was busy making an execution block and a hurdle upon which to draw the three man to the gallows. All the preparations were ready and on November 8th the execution took place in public. Among the people who witnessed the proceedings was the poet Shelley. He wrote a pamphlet called *"We pity the plumage but forget the dying bird,"* which compares this death with Princess Charlotte's who died the day before in childbirth.

The three, Brandreth, Turner and Ludlam, were hung and left dangling for over half an hour. Each was then taken down in turn and the executioner used his new axes to behead them. The name of the executioner was never revealed and his face was hidden under a black mask. He was chosen especially for his accuracy in using a pick-axe in a nearby mine. The mutilated remains of the three were buried the same day, without any service, in a communal grave at St. Werburgh's Church in Derby. The block used for this execution can be seen in the Derby museum.

Stocks

Although used in Roman times and mentioned in the Bible, stocks were not introduced into English Law until 1351 when Edward the third had the following section entered into the Statutes of the Realm: "And that those which refuse to make such Oath (to observe the Law) shall be put in the stocks by the said Lords. And the stocks be made in every town for such occasions." One of the best examples to be seen in Derbyshire is the stocks opposite Eyam Hall on the village green.

In the seventeenth century a further act became law: *"That every person convicted of drunkenness should be fined 5s.(25p) or spend six hours in the stock."* In 1703 a James

Crozier of Bakewell wilfully broke the stocks, his sentence was to occupy them as soon as they were repaired. In 1685 Joseph Snow was convicted for drunkenness and violence and was sentenced to occupy the village stocks at Pentrich for three successive afternoons.

Miner's Punishment

A singularly savage Derbyshire punishment. If a person stole from a lead mine in Edward's reign (Edward 1st 1271-1307), his punishment was to have his hand nailed to a table and no food placed near him. The miner either had to starve to death or saw his nailed hand off and attain his freedom.

Whipping

A common punishment which was a regular occurrence. Here are three typical entries of this sentence from the Order of Sessions of Derby:

> *1684 - "Ordered that Samuel Levesly and William Bennet Jnr. both convicted for petty larceny to be delivered over to the custody of the Master of the House of Correction, in Derby, there to remain for the space of one month, during which time he is required by this court to punish them by whipping and keeping them to hard labour. And to allow them no more maintenance than what they shall get by their labour."*

> *1708—"Cutberd Rogerson and Mary, his wife, both found guilty, this sessions of petty larceny ordered both to be whipped through the market, to be stripped to the waist and whipped at a cart from one end of the town of Wirksworth unto the other."*

> *1729—"A man convicted at the Epitaph Sessions, for sheep stealing and to be publicly whipped at Derby, between the hours of 12 a.m. and 1 p.m. the next three market days."*

In the eighteenth century women were supposed to be whipped in private, but in Bakewell in 1735 two women were flogged naked to the waist In 1791 a law was introduced abolishing the whipping of females.

Pillory

Another popular punishment, for it meant that one could get rid of old rotten food and hurl it at the defenceless occupier! Usually a person who was about to serve a a three or six month prison sentence would occupy the pillory for an hour. This punishment was abolished by Queen Victoria on June 30th, 1837.

"You find the pillory is your fate, With dirt and rotten eggs, avat thy pate."

There is one interesting example which concerns a Mrs. Beare who, having attempted but failed to poison her husband in 1732, was instructed to stand in the pillory in Derby for two market days. On the first day eggs and turnips were thrown at her, but after a few minutes she wriggled out and escaped into the crowd, only to be taken back to jail. The second time she reached the pillory she kneeled down to beg for mercy. The officers took no notice and manhandled her into position, but her head would not go through the hole. After removing her hat they found a pewter plate which they threw to the crowd. They then placed her in position. The crowd showed no mercy, eggs, turnips and potatoes being thrown. Only when blood began to run down the pillory did they ease their deluge. When she finally found the sanctuary of the jail, "those who saw her afterwards in the gaol said she was such an object as she was not fit to be looked upon."

The Brank

This is a most fascinating punishment, which no doubt many men wish was around today. It was known as the Gossip Bridle or Scolder's Bridle. The Brank was an adjustable metal frame which fitted over a woman's head and was designed to stop her from talking. If she did attempt to speak, a sharp projection which fitted into the mouth, and often had spikes on, would lacerate her tongue. Consequently, all her friends and enemies could call her all the rude names they liked, knowing she was unable to reply.

A woman to receive such a punishment would have to raise her voice in public or spread rumours about a local eminent person. The woman would be paraded through the streets and tied in the pillory or to the market cross. There was only one in Derbyshire, at Chesterfield. and it was made in 1688. Although extensively used in other counties, the reason for its lack of use in Derbyshire was, as one seventeenth century writer so aptly wrote, *"The country women here are chaste and sober, and very diligent in their housewifery; they hate idleness, love and obey their husbands."*

The Ducking Stool

Another punishment for women. Generally it was a wooden beam, pivoted in the middle. At one end, hanging from a chain, was a chair, and at the other a cord. The woman sat in the chair and by operation of the cord could he ducked in a stream at the operator's discretion. There was one in Derby suspended over the Markeaton

Brook and another in Chesterfield. The latter one was taken down at the beginning of the nineteenth century, and it is believed to have been last used in 1790. Generally the punish ment was two duckings. On the occasion of its last use the woman, on rising from her second ducking, let out a stream of rude words The operator then ducked her again, keeping her under a little longer. When she came out she did not utter a single word.

Sentence now hear this. you are to be whipped through the market, to be stripped to the waist and whipped at a cart from one end of Wirksworth unto the other.

GIBBETING

Gibbeting was a gruesome aftermath of hanging, Until the late eighteenth century a person who had committed murder was liable, after being hung, to have his body placed on a post and fixed to it by chains. There it hung upon the site of the murder to act as a reminder to people as to what would happen if they committed a crime. Gibbeting also brought disgrace to the family name. As a further deterrent to committing a wrong doing there was a reward of £100 to anyone who provided sufficient evidence to cause a person to be hanged.

There are three places in the Peak District which incorporate the word Gibbet. Gibbet Rocks, near Loxley Edge (Grid Ref. 305892), is where a young lad of eighteen was murdered by a person named Frank Fearn. The other two are in Derbyshire—Gibbet Moor to the east of Chatsworth (Grid Ref. 282707), and Gibbet Field near Wardlow Mires (Grid Ref. 181757).

> "After having walked eleven hours without having traced the print of a human foot, to my great comfort and delight, I saw a man hanging upon a gibbet: my pleasure at the cheering prospect was inexpressible, for it convinced me that I was in a civilised country!"
> A true and alarming piece of writing from a member of one of Sir Francis Drake's voyages to South America.

The murder on Gibbet Moor, which led to the moor being called after it, is a very morbid tale indeed. A woman was frying some bacon inside her cottage. While in the process of preparing this tasty meal for herself, a tramp knocked at the door and asked for some food. She replied she did not supply scroungers like him with food. He again asked her, for he could smell bacon frying, and again she refused. Losing his temper, he attacked her and after a few moments became so enraged that he picked up the frying pan full of hot fat and poured it down her throat, scalding her to death. The tramp was soon arrested for his crime and the magistrate ruled that he must he gibbeted alive and hung from the cottage door. There he hung through all kinds of weather, yelling and screaming, as he slowly died. His screams could be heard by the Duke of Devonshire at Chatsworth, and it was he who made sure that no one was ever again gibbeted alive in Derbyshire.

The tale of the Gibbet Field, near Wardlow, is another sad story, but it does have a happy ending. The Minstrel of the Peak William Newton, was horrified at this gibbet, which made him write a lengthy poem about it. This poem played a large part in the abolishment of gibbeting.

Wardlow Mires was a toll house and the junction point for the roads from Stoney Middleton and Bakewell. One day a large crowd had accumulated, impatiently waiting for the toll keeper to come and collect their dues and let them through. The noise of stamping horses, men shouting and blasts on a bugle brought the barmaid from the nearby inn to see what was happening. Not seeing the toll keeper, Hannah Oliver, she went to the keeper's house, but as she neared the doorway she was stunned to see a lifeless body hanging over the doorstep. Hannah had been murdered.

The police were soon at the scene. They carried out a thorough examination and interviewed everyone close by, but nothing would give them a lead. The only odd part about the case was a pair of red shoes which were missing from Hannah's feet. The shoes had quite an adventure until one day the murderer, Anthony Lingard although not connected with the murder at this stage, was acting in a suspicious manner. The police questioned him and also searched his room. In one of the drawers was the pair of shoes. He had at first given these to a girl friend, who could not accept them because she wondered where he had obtained the money to buy them. So Lingard received the shoes back. To rid himself of them he placed them in a haystack, but a few days later he removed them and took them home.

The police were now suspicious of Lingard, but had insufficient evidence to arrest him. Fortunately they knew who had made the shoes, a Mr. Marsden of Stoney Middleton. To ascertain for whom they were made, Mr. Marsden, although he recognised the shoes, had to strip one down completely. He knew that inside he had incorporated a piece of packing with the motto, "Commit no Crime," written on. He found this and confirmed they were Hannah Oliver's, thus sealing Lingard's fate.

The trial was held in Derby and the verdict was that Lingard should be hung and then gibbeted at the scene of the crime. Here at the age of twenty-one, and from April 1st, 1815, his body hung for several months, the cost of the gibbeting being £85. The first evening the gibbet was erected a sermon was preached beneath it. Many of the toll keepers frequently complained about the eerie noise of bones rattling in the wind! When it was finally taken down the skull was sent to Belle Vue, Manchester, where it was put on show to the public This was the last gibbet in Derbyshire, and we must thank William Newton for his moving poem about Lingard's father who came alone on the first night to see his son's body. The poem is set at midnight with a storm raging the area. Newton titled it, *"The supposedly soliloquy of a father under the Gibbet of his son, upon one of the Peak Mountains, near Ward low."*

His poem opens -

> *"Art thou, my Son, suspended here on high,*
> *— Ah! What a sight to meet a Father's eye!*
> *To see what most I prized, what most I loved,*
> *What most I cherished,—and once approved,*
> *Hung in mid air to feed the nauseous worm,*
> *And waving horrid in the midnight storm!"*

He concludes:

> *"If crime demand it, let the offender die,*
> *But let no more the Gibbet brave the sky;*
> *No more let vengeance on the dead be hurled,*
> *But hide the victim from a gazing world."*

His ending is most apt and is what did eventually happen, but I wonder, did Newton believe this would come about as a result of his poem?

DOG-WHIPPER & SLUGGARD WAKER

The church wardens in the seventeenth and eighteenth centuries had many more duties than they have today. It was their job to maintain the church building and property, and see to the payments for this work. At services, as they do today, they allocated seats and kept order during the proceedings. If you look through the old church wardens' accounts and parish registers, you will come across the following two unusual aspects of church life.

Dog-Whipper

Shortly before the service the official dog-whipper would use his whip and drive out all the dogs from the inside of the church. At St. Ann s Church, Baslow, just inside the main door on the wall on your left is a glass fronted case containing a dog whip. The lash is about three feet long and secured to a short stout stick of ash with leather round the handle.

These accounts are of interest:

Youlgreave Parish Church

> *1609 To Robert Walton for whipping y dogges forth of y church in tyme of divine service ... ... 1/4d. (6p)*

> *1617 To Robert Benbowe for whipping out y dogges 2/0d.(10p)*

> *1715 For a coat and furniture for y dog-whipper ... 11/6d. (52p)*

Eyam Parish Church

> *1727 February 1st. Buried George Newton de Eyam. Dog Whipper.*

> *1748 February 5th. Buried Stephen Broomhead. Dog Whipper de Eyam, who had been overlaid in y snow upon Eyam Moor.*

Other accounts record that the official dog-whipper received an annual salary of 8s.(40p), while another records the fee of 2s.(10p) paid to a wife for doing the task.

Sluggard Waker

This is an even more unusual duty. His aim was to keep drowsy members of the congregation awake by tapping them on the head with a long wand. In Castleton, in 1722, 10s.(50p) was paid to the Sluggard Waker. The design of the wand varied. Some were just straight pieces of wood, while another type had a forked end which could be adjusted to fit the culprit's neck and hence to shake the victim. But the best one of all had a fox's tail at one end and a solid knob of wood at the other. The tail was used to gently tickle the faces of the female sleepers, and the male offenders received a sharp tap on the head with the knob end.

LOST LAD

On the Ordnance Survey Outdoor Leisure map - The Dark Peak, to the right of Derwent Reservoir and near the summit of Back Tor, are the words "Lost Lad (Grid Ref. 193912). The tale behind the name is the story of a young teenage boy who lost his way. There are two tales of how he became lost, but both end in the same manner.

The First Tale

...Abraham lived with his mother in the old village of Derwent which now lies submerged under the Ladybower Reservoir. His father died when he was very young, leaving his mother to run their small farm As he grew older Abraham became a strong youth, capable of doing most jobs on the farm, although the one from which he derived the most pleasure was attending the sheep. One winter the weather had been particularly atrocious with high winds and heavy falls of snow, and before long the village was cut off from the outside world.

One day the weather cleared, and on his mother's instructions Abraham set off up towards Derwent Edge to locate the sheep and, with the aid of his dog, bring them down to the farm. He liked the idea of going out into this white landscape and had a tremendous feeling of adventure as his boots crunched in the fresh snow. His mother stood in the doorway, watching him ascend the valley side until he disappeared from view. From Derwent Edge he did not have far to go before he could see several of his sheep. So engrossed was he in his task of rounding them all together that he failed to notice the change in the weather. It began to snow and before long dense mist obliterated the familiar landmarks. However he struggled on, gathering his sheep, but every time the mist cleared for a brief second he could not recognise the country around him.

After several hours of walking he knew he was lost, so finding a shelter underneath a rock he crawled in and waited for the snow storm to end. Cold penetrated his limbs and tiredness racked his brain. Before falling asleep he picked up a stone and scratched the words "Lost Lad" on the rock. He fell asleep, tired, hungry and cold, never to awake again. It is believed that the faithful dog remained with his master until he too died. His mother below was heartbroken. She kept watch from the window all night long, hoping against hope that he would return.

Richard Furness, "The Parnassus of the Peak", wrote a poem *"A Tale of Derwent"*, part of which is:

> *Ere this his mother, o'er the moorland hill,*
> *Foreboded Abraham lost, or many an ill,*

As anxiously, or ere the clock struck four,
She gazed till her eyes could gaze no more.
"He comes not still!" she said, "tis dark, no moon!
Oh! woe betide me, if comes not soon.
Why did I let him go?

At the first glow of dawn his mother alerted all her neighbours, who quickly donned their clothing and set off to search for Abraham. The recent snow-storm had erased his tracks and although they searched until dusk no trace could be found.

Three months later, in early spring, a shepherd was walking near Back Tor when he passed a rock with "Lost Lad" freshly marked upon it. He stopped, and on closer inspection found the remains of Abraham. From then on, for at least one hundred years, every shepherd who passed his resting place put a stone on the site. Eventually a large cairn marked the spot.

The Other Tale

...In the early sixteenth century a young boy, aged about thir teen, loved to wander and chase animals in the Derwent Valley. His father was a forester. Frequently these trips up the valley were long and arduous, causing parental concern. One bright morning he set off and was soon enjoying himself, but tragically his enthusiasm ran away with him for he ventured further afield than ever before. By late afternoon he was lost and extremely tired. Fear of the dark now gripped him, making him run in any direction until darkness blackened the countryside. Finally he collapsed on to the heatherland and fell into an exhausted sleep.

His parents were alarmed at his non-return and spent most of the night wandering near their home, calling his name. His father walked miles searching for him, all night and all next day. Meanwhile, with the dawn the boy rose, ate a few wild berries and ascended the nearest high point, hoping to see some recognisable feature. Alas, nothing was familiar to him. He walked on, ascending hillocks and descending shallow dales, while his body was racked with hunger and tiredness. His father, too, continued looking for a few days, but realised that he must have perished some where in that vast moorland mass. The boy wandered around aimlessly, hoping for a miracle for the next seven days. Finally he ascended Back Tor, but no familiar scene met his eyes. Near ing collapse he found a rock which offered some kind of shelter and here he went to sleep. Before doing so he marked the rock with the words "Lost Lad" and built a small cairn. That night his little heart stopped. Here his body remained for many years, long after the death of his parents. A group of people were walking in the area and came across this sad memorial, the words on the stone being just decipherable. The cairn is quite large and can still be seen today. Of the two tales, both of which arc tragically sorrowful, I prefer the former; it has a more authentic ring to it.

THE BATTLE OF WIN HILL
AND LOSE HILL

Looking at the map of the Peak District, one sees these two hills on the right-hand side of the Hope Valley above the village of Hope. But one never questions how or why they came to be so christened—at least I didn't! The answer stares you in the face; an army assembled on each hill and after the battle one was the loser and the other the winner! There is no authoritative account of the battle, and we can only conjecture that the follow ing is the tale.

The battle took place over 1,300 years ago between the kings of Wessex and Northumbria. There had been friction between these two for some time. Ceolwulf, the King of Wessex, died in 626 A.D. and left his kingdom to be divided between his two sons Cynegils and Cuichelm. Shortly before Ceolwulf's death, Edwin, King of Northumbria, had taken some of his land and used it for his own purpose. Ceolwulf knew of the might of Edwin and, being inferior in strength, he did not threaten him. But Cuichelm now planned a subtle way to secure his father's revenge. He sent an envoy, named Eumer, to see Edwin. When Eumer was finally given an audience, he waited until they were close before he drew a double-edged dagger and thrust it at Edwin's heart. Tragically, Eumer's movements had been watched by Lilla, a beautiful maid-servant of Edwin. Seeing Eumer about to strike her king, she stepped between them and received the mortal blow in her heart, falling dead at their feet. Immediately the whole room was in a state of chaos—servants attending to Lilla and trying to revive her; guards surrounding Edwin for protection; and the largest group busy killing Eumer for his attempted assassination. Before Eumer died, Edwin learned that Cuichelm was the planner of this deed. Leaving Eumer to die from over a hundred wounds, he issued orders to his chiefs that they were marching on Cuichelm.

News spread quickly to Cuichelm about the approaching army. His brother Cynegils and himself had a mutual agreement that if either was in trouble the other would come and give assistance. While the two brothers assembled their two armies, Penda, King of Mercia, heard about the forthcoming battle. Being jealous of Edwin's power, Penda quickly gathered his men and joined the two brothers in their march towards Edwin. When the two armies were near each other Edwin approached the two hills. Seeing that Win Hill was the highest he and his men made it their base, camp ing on the summit. The next day Edwin was horrified to see the huge army from Wessex approach and take over Lose Hill; there seemed to be one endless stream of men. Seeing such a multitude he ordered his men to build a stone wall, with breaks, around the perimeter of the summit plateau, the idea of the breaks being to permit a hasty retreat. That night both armies clustered around their respective summits beside roaring wood fires.

At sunrise each army dispatched an ambassador down to the banks of the river Noe, about midway between the two hills. This was a formal procedure and was one of the rules of the game. Cuichelm's representative said to Edwin's: *"Robber of my father's inheritance, this day thou shalt his son's proud vengeance feel! Come forth with thy chiefs and let this gushing stream of the vale witness the might and strength which justice ever yields!"*

Edwin's envoy replied: *"Perfidious wretch! Dost thou boast of justice? Hast thou not another assassin at thy command to effect a coward's purpose? Vain boaster, ere night this stream shall leave its sandy bed and flow among the mangled remains of thy dishonoured dead!"*

Further exchanges passed between them before they retired and reported to their kings as to what had transpired. With wild shouts and brandishing their swords in the air, both armies descended towards each other and battle commenced.

A. G. Jewitt in 1815 published a three-part poem on the Peak District called *The Wanderings of Memory*. A few verses relate to this battle, the first verse being:

> *You hills were witness to the well fought day*
> *They saw our phalanx stand in grim array,*
> *They heard each warrior strike the pounding shield,*
> *And dare the invading legions to the field.*
> *The din of battle through the dale resounds*
> *With every blow the list'ning rocks rebounds.*

The battle was indeed bloody, and in a very short time the river Noe was crimson. Neither side gained an advantage for as soon as one side pushed the other back it was in turn repulsed. Edwin was often in the thickets, swinging his great sword into the Wessex men, but much later in the day the superior numbers of the Wessex army began to push Edwin back. He saw this as his chance and upon a signal his men backed and ran up the hill. Wessex's men, seeing them flee, followed with victory in their mouths, but before they could stop they realised their folly. As soon as Edwin's army was behind the wall it began to heave the boulders down on to the Wessex army. The Wessex men were powerless, and as the boulders cascaded down most of the army was destroyed. Edwin's messenger had prophesied correctly; the river did leave its sandy bed and swirl around Wessex's mutilated men! Cuichelm, his brother and Penda beat a hasty retreat back to Wessex with their remaining men. Edwin, although he lost over half his men, returned to Northumbria triumphant with his revenge for the murder of Lilla accomplished.

A. G. Jewitt concludes his poem:

How are the mighty fallen! The sounding bow,
The sword and quivering spear are perished now;
The strong arm'd chieftain, once his country's trust,
Is lost in silence, mingled with the dust,
You stony hillocks rising mark his bed,
There, for their native hills our warriors bled,
And yet to unborn years those mounds shall tell,
Where free men bravely fought, where Britons nobly fell.

THE WINNATS MURDER

Peak Forest was once the Gretna Green of England. In April 1758 a young couple who had come down from Scotland were almost at their destination when a group of five miners ambushed them in Winnats Pass, ruthlessly murdered them and robbed them of their money. The crime was not discovered until the last of the five murderers confessed on his death-bed some twenty years later.

The young lovers were called Allan and Clara; their surnames no one knows. Some of the early nineteenth century writers named them Helen and Clara, one of them, Mr. A. G. Jewitt of Rotherham, writing a very long poem called The Wanderings of Memory or Buxton and the Peak, published for private distribution in 1815. In it is a Peak ballad, *"Henry and Clara,"* and being so well written, I have interwoven a selection of verses to help tell this sad tale.

Clara's parents were adamantly against their marriage. The couple met in private at night, but often one of Clara's brothers intercepted Allan on his mission and threatened him with a gun. They could not keep up this undercover affair any longer, so Allan summoned up his courage and went to see Clara's father to ask for his consent.

> *Dar'd to ask the wealthy lordling,*
> *For the damsel's willing hand—*
>
> *Pleaded with respectful fervour,*
> *Who could his request withstand?*
>
> *Clara's father—he—withstood it,*
> *He the ardent suit denied—*
>
> *To a house so poor, though noble*
> *Never would he be allied.*

His refusal left them no alternative but to run away, so deep and pure was their love. In the middle of the night, on the prearranged date, they met and set off towards happiness. Their route was long and passed through out-of-the-way places, in their hope that should they be pursued the trackers would not locate them. In time they neared their goal and arrived, shortly after dawn, in the village of Stoney Middleton. Again, trying to be inconspicuous, they chose a lower class inn called the Royal Oak. Inside the place was in a chaotic mess after the previous night's fight, but the innkeeper made them welcome. Leaving them to sit in a room she hurriedly prepared a drink, while for food Allan unpacked one of the saddlebags which contained a little to eat. He reflected how miserable Clara seemed, and on enquiry she revealed the nightmare she had during the night. It was so life like and real that she had grave misgivings about continuing.

Clara's dream was about themselves. While on the journey they entered an awesome dale, and part way through were attacked and robbed. Allan was murdered before her eyes, and when the attackers came towards her she woke up! Allan tried in vain to reassure her that it was only a dream. However they continued to Castleton, following the route described by the innkeeper.

In Castleton they stopped at another inn. Inside they sat in the best room while opposite a group of rowdy miners were, much to their displeasure, being thrown out by the landlord. Here the lovers whiled away a couple of hours before remounting and setting off on the final leg to Peak Forest via the Winnats Pass. The four miners had noticed the couple at the inn and taken note of their apparently rich state Feeling sore at being turned out the four men, James Ashton, Nicholas Cook, Thomas Hall and Francis Butler, set off for Odin Mine. On the way one of them suggested robbing the couple who had just arrived at the inn, and the more it was discussed the more attractive the idea became. By the time they reached the mine their minds were made up. At the mine was their fellow workman John Bradshaw, who was threatened with a pickaxe, and reluctantly came with them. Quickly they walked over to the pass and waited for the couple.

As they entered, Clara was very apprehensive about continuing for the setting was so like her dream, but Allan laughed at her stupidity and on they went. About halfway it happened. Out leapt the five men and within seconds the riders were forced to dis mount. Clara fainted, muttering *"My dream, my dream."*

In that glen so dark and dismal,
Five ruffians met this youthful pair;
Long the lover bravely struggled,
Fought to save his bride so fair.

One of the miners had a barn close by so they manhandled the couple into it. After repeated demands Allan relinquished their money which amounted to £200. Leaving the couple inside the miners went outside to discuss what to do next, Allan soothing Clara and trying to restore her confidence that they would be all right. On the miners' return both Allan and Clara pleaded for each other's lives, but the five stared at them making no move or sound. Allan could not stand this battle of nerves any longer and so flew into them with fists flying within seconds he was overpowered and

High they lift the murderous weapon,
Wretches hear ye not her cries?
High they lift the murderous weapon,

Lo! her love, her husband dies.

Clara stared at Allan's body, lifeless on the floor, killed by a blow from a pickaxe. She looked up at the murderers and pleaded for her life, asking to be stripped and sent out naked. But her words were of no use:

> *High they lift the murderous weapon,*
> *Who can bide her piercing shriek?*
> *Tis done—the dale is wrapt in silence,*
> *On their hands the life-blood reeks.*

Until dusk the miners sat in the barn, barely speaking, and realising the change in their lives through this brutal action. When darkness came they dispersed and agreed to meet later to bury the bodies. About midnight they returned, but the pass looked intimidating and when they neared the barn a noise frightened them away. The same applied the following night, but on the third when the same happened again Ashton said, "It was only the devil; he would not hurt them! " Gaining confidence, they wrapped the two bodies in a sack and buried them. The job completed, the miners divided the money equally and parted.

The horses were found on the fourth day, but everyone assumed that the couple had been murdered and the bodies thrown down Eldon Hole. The horses, after no one claimed them, went to Chatsworth. One Sunday shortly afterwards one of the miners' daughters appeared at church with an expensive dress on; it is believed to have been Clara's, removed from her body just prior to burial. Although public justice was never administered, the five murderers lived miserable lives. James Ashton, with his share of the money, bought a few horses which soon died. He was the person who related the murder on his death-bed, his conscience troubling him so much that he could not die until he had told the story. Nicholas Cook was walking near the site of the crime when he fell from one of the buttresses and was instantly killed. Thomas Hall became so dejected that he hanged himself. John Bradshaw walked up the pass one day, and when close to the scene a stone hit him on the head and killed him. Finally, Francis Butler drove himself mad with continually remembering the murders. He often tried to commit suicide, but he was unsuccessful until he died naturally but miserable. While digging in a mine shaft in the pass some ten years after the crime, the excavators came across two skeletons which were believed to be Allan's and Clara's. Clara's saddle can be seen in the shop beside Speedwell Cavern at the entrance to the pass.

> *Christians, I have told my ditty,*
> *If you shudder not with fear,*
> *If your breast can glow with pity,*
> *Can you now withhold a tear?*

DERBYSHIRE'S GRETNA GREEN

During the years between 1728-1754, Peak Forest was a place where anyone could be married immediately and at any time of the day or night. The vicars were under no jurisdiction from any bishop, had no superior to report to, and consequently took advantage of these unique circumstances. Not only did they issue marriage licences but also stamped documents with their own seal and granted probate to wills. The vicar also held the title of *Principal Official and Judge in Spiritualities in the Peculiar Court of Peak Forest.*

Peak Forest was so named as it was the centre of the Royal Deer Forest which William Peveril of Peveril Castle created in 1100. The Head Forester originally lived here, and there existed a farmhouse called Dogman's Slack where the person in charge of the hounds lived. It was a very wild and bleak spot, and was not frequented by many.

The chapel where the marriages took place was financed by the Duchess of Devonshire and built in 1657, the Devonshire family owning it for several years before conveying it by deed as a gift to the minister. The Duchess had the chapel erected as an act of loyalty to King Charles the first who was executed, her son serving in his army. The chapel was built on the west side of the present churchyard and dedicated to *"Charles, King and Martyr."* It was dismantled in 1880 and the stones were used to build a reading room on the right-hand side of the present church which also dates from 1880. The font came from the original chapel; if you look among the gravestones you will find a stone pillar about two feet high which is the base of the font in its position in the chapel.

The news of this "marriage" state soon percolated through the area and in time became known about all over England. It was not until 1728 that anyone came and took advantage of this service, but with the commencement of these "foreign marriages" as they were called, the vicar made a special register for them. In 1728 there were only 18 marriages, but on average over the next 26 years they worked out at about one a week. The two busiest years were in 1745, with 105, and 1746 with 92. On average 75% of the marriages took place during the summer months and approximately 70% came from a 50-mile radius of Peak Forest.

The vicar earned about £100 per year for the service. One writer wrote: *"'Pay and marry, say nothing and go away,' appeared to be a profitable and veritable golden rule of the merry vicars of nearly 200 years ago!"* Unfortunately we do not have any account of what transpired in the chapel. We can only envisage a couple of lovers arriving in the middle of the night, wakening the vicar, paying a fee and going to the chapel to be married before their parents came to stop the service. Not all people were fortunate, for Allan and Clara were murdered before they reached the vicarage. (See The Winnats Murder.)

The foreign marriage register was ended thus: *"Here endeth the list of persons who came from different parishes in England and were married at Peak Forest. This was a privilege of the Minister, but being productive probably of bad consequences was put a stop to, by an Act of Parliament."* (Hugh Wolstenholm. July 1804.) The Act was a result of parents and guardians being alarmed at the easy way one could get married, not only at Peak Forest, but by the "Fleet Marriages" which were taking place in London. Lord Hardwick's Act was passed through Parliament in 1753 and came into force on March 25th, 1754.

However this is not the end of the tale. for one can still get married at Peak Forest without banns. The only stipulation is that one of the parties must live in the village for at least fifteen consecutive days prior to the ceremony, and the service must take place in the daytime. Even in this century people have come to be married immediately. A column in the Sheffield Telegraph on Wednesday, 13th April, 1938, was headed:

Wanted Quick Wedding.
Peak Forest Vicar says No.

This young couple, although rebuffed, stayed the night in the village and the following day again attempted to be married, but again the vicar said no!

In April 1938 there was quite a lot of controversy over weddings at Peak Forest, even to the extent of involving the Bishop of Derby. The Bishop stated that "no irregularity had been reported to him, and he did not propose to take any action." The vicar too was under pressure and in the Sheffield Telegraph he was reported as saying: "I have been criticised because of these so-called secret weddings. They are not secret. Anyone can come to the church and watch the marriage. But I am certainly not going to shout it all over the place that a wedding is taking place in my church." In 1946 a couple came to be married immediately, but again the vicar refused, advising them that they were too young.

The marriage certificates were stamped by a wooden seal which dates back to 1661. It has two ends; one oval which has a Latin inscription around symbols of the passion, crown of thorns and the three nails of the cross. The inscription means *"Seal of the Jurisdiction of St. Charles the first Martyr."* The other end is round and depicts forest figures with Latin words around the periphery referring to the date when the forest was created in 1100A.D.

DAFT SAMMY OF CASTLETON

Samuel Eyre, for much of the first half of the nineteenth century, was one of the sights of Castleton. How he acquired the title of "Daft Sammy" is a mystery, for he should have been called "Clever Sammy." He certainly had his head screwed on the right way, although his type of job was rather revolutionary at that time.

He was born in 1806, from simple parents. As soon as he was old enough to work he went into lead mining, virtually the only job except farming in the area. He was deeply in love with Castleton and soon became an authority on its delights, places to see, caverns, vantage points and local gossip. As time passed he became so involved with Castleton that he had to tell everyone about its attributes. While working at the lead mine he would often see a stagecoach coming on its way to Castleton. Dropping his tools, he would run to meet it and tell the occupants about the village. On several occasions he was more than handsomely rewarded.

He soon realised that with his knowledge, and the obvious interest in the village, he could earn a living by being a guide. The decision made, he put away his mining tools for good and began establishing himself as the unofficial guide to Castleton. His favourite tour was Peveril Castle. Although he never asked for any fee for taking people around, he was invariably given a few coppers. He also kept a careful watch on who came into the village. If ever anyone wanted to know who was there, Sammy would know. He kept watch for his own livelihood, and would follow folk wherever they went in the village until they had to give him some money. Having paid, he left them alone to enjoy the wonders of the locality.

He was always most helpful on any guided tour, showing his party the best vantage points and taking the easiest path. While he led the way he would recount the various colourful tales and gossip of Castleton to help people enjoy the walk. He would also add, when near the end of the trip, how generous the last party had been. With the fairer sex he was God's gift to women. What ever was asked of him he did. Weight or size was of no con sequence; if a damsel wanted carrying across a river he would oblige.

Perhaps his most helpful stunt was on the steep road up past Mam Tor. When a stagecoach came to ascend this particular stretch the majority of people climbed out of the coach, as they felt safer walking up than riding. Here Sammy showed his strength, forming all the passengers in a line and with each one holding another's hand, pulling them up. His coat was a maze of patches of varying sizes and colours. This was a result of this service, for several people clung to his coat which ripped under the strain.

One day his mother, with whom he lived, joined one of his parties. A member asked him who she was and he replied: *"Oh, it's some poor old woman or other; give her sixpence."*

What little money he had he always kept in his hand, even when he was asleep in his sack. He was never known to lend anyone even a copper, except on one occasion. He happened to be at the Blue John Mine near Mam Tor when the attendant, a Mr. Tym, asked if Sammy had ten shillings he could borrow as he had run out of loose change. Mr. Tym did not expect for one moment that Sammy had any, but since he was desperate for change he felt he should ask. Much to his amazement Sammy lent him the money in sixpenny pieces. Having handed the money over he did not let Mr. Tym out of his sight. When he was given the ten shillings back in the form of a half-sovereign, Sammy took a lot of convincing that it was equal to the twenty pieces he had originally lent.

He had a large appetite and could devour large quantities in a short period of time. Several of the villagers took pity on him and saved all the "leftovers" each day for him. At Christmas he was a particular nuisance, for on the pretext of singing a carol he would stay in the house until he was given either some money or food. Once having been given something, he always quietly slipped away and moved into the next. He never went to school nor ever had any schooling. He was proud of this, for he boasted that he could spell and sing. His favourite word, with which he took delight in showing vocabulary knowledge, was "brazen." He spelt it BRAUZZETT-EN. His singing was even worse, hopelessly out of tune and with a croaky voice. But to his credit he always concluded his musical recital with God Save the King.

Regretfully, like everyone else, he grew old and did not have the strength to ascend the slope to the castle or to take a party to some nearby viewpoint. Instead, he spent most of the day smoking his pipe at the base of the castle. When anyone came by with the intention of seeing the building he informed them that they paid him here. Being unable to support himself any longer he went to live in the workhouse at Chapel-en-le-Frith, but after a month he died peacefully on 30th January, 1868. With no one to pay for a tombstone, the villagers of Castleton held a concert in the village to raise money for one. Sufficient was gathered and a tombstone worthy of him was erected in the churchyard. Although the letters have become illegible by weathering, it did contain the following, which if he knew what was written, makes a worthy ending to this likable character of Castleton.

> *"Sacred to the memory of Samuel Eyre, known by the name of Sammy Scutt or Daft Sammy. He was born of parents in humble life and supported himself the greater portion of his life by acting as guide to Castleton."*

THE EYAM PLAGUE

There are several "must" inclusions in a book dealing with the historical side of Derbyshire. The plague which struck the village of Eyam in 1665-66 is one of them. The following story is one without parallel in its tragic and often heart-rending terror.

Mompesson. the central figure, was born in 1638 from a Wiltshire family who originated in Normandy—hence his French surname. He was for a while chaplain to Sir George Saville, who in due course offered him the post of rector at Eyam which he took in 1664. The previous rector was the Rev. Thomas Stanley, who was the incumbent for eighteen years, but when the Corporation Act of 1661 was introduced he would not conform to it. Consequently he had to relinquish his post and Mompesson took over but instead of leaving the village Stanley stayed. A year later when the village was under the grip of the plague, the Rev. Stanley became Mompesson's right-hand man.

The arrival of the plague is generally acknowledged to have taken place in September 1665. Close to the church is a row of cottages now known as the *"Plague Cottages."* One of them was owned by the Cooper family, and living with them was a tailor called George Vicars. A parcel of clothes had been sent to him from London in September. Vicars opened the parcel and noted that the contents were damp, so he dried them in front of the fire. In doing so the plague vapours filtered through the household — a few days later he died and shortly afterwards all the Cooper family contracted the disease; the only person of the household to survive was Mrs. Cooper. At first no one paid much attention to the deaths, but with six by the end of September people became suspicious. In October, 23 people caught the disease and died.

The population of Eyam, a healthy lead mining village, at this time was approximately 1,000. Villagers with friends in neighbouring counties quickly left and a population of 350 remained as a result of entreaties by Mompesson. *"What Mompesson did was to persuade his people with some show of resignation to remain in the village. He gave them consolation, he inspired them with hope. He brought them up to that fine exaltation of spirit which nerved them to face death as disciplined sailors face it in shipwreck— he made the manifest duty of self-sacrifice appear reasonable."*

Mompesson also successfully sent his children, George and Elizabeth, away. He also pleaded with his wife, Catherine, to go, but she would not leave, saying that her place was by his side. With the reduced number in the village, Mompesson secured their loyalty to isolation from the outside world, thus confining the plague to Eyam. He drew an imaginary line a mile in diameter around the village, as the limits of the inhabitants' wanderings, there being five points on this line where other villages left food. Mompesson had written to the Earl of Devonshire asking for help, and this was assured. Some of the Earl's men kept watch around the line and provisions and medical supplies were left at a certain point, now known as Mompesson's Well. Mompesson would leave money in the water (which was sprinkled with vinegar to avoid spreading the disease) in return for the supplies. A note was also left, informing the Earl of the number of deaths and generally of the state of the village.

In spite of the watch kept on the village, several people entered and some tried to escape. One woman escaped to Tideswell, having successfully answered questions by a guard. However, in Tideswell she was recognised as an "Eyam woman" and many of the inhabitants hurled eggs, grass sods and rotten fruit at her until she left. One person who came into the village was a carter from Bubnell Against the wishes of his village, he loaded his cart with wood and went to Eyam where, in pouring rain, he unloaded the wood by himself. Two days later he was ill and from the appearance he seemed to have the plague symptoms. The news leaked out and the little village was in a state of unrest, fearing the worst. The Earl of Devonshire learnt about the villagers' peril and summoned a doctor who interviewed his patient across the river Derwent, thus eliminating further contamination. From the interview the doctor diagnosed a severe cold and a few days later the carter was up and about, much to everyone's relief.

From November 1665 to May 1666 no more than nine villagers a month died from the disease, bringing the total to 77 deaths in nine months. The next five months were to see almost treble that number. To reduce further contamination, Mompesson stopped holding his services in the church. Instead, he chose a quiet little dale close by called the "Delf" Part way up it is a rock from where he preached, this open air church being known as the Cucklet Church. Two services were held on Sunday and during the week there was a short service most days. But as the months progressed, his congregation grew smaller and smaller.

In June 1666 the number of deaths rose sharply, 19 being recorded. July was even worse with 56. A villager named Marshall Howe had assumed the responsibilities of gravedigger—for payment he would ransack the diseased person's house. Some people were buried in the churchyard, but many were buried close to the farms or in fields near the village.

August saw the village in complete turmoil, for the number of deaths rose alarmingly to 77. One of the most tragic cases was the Hancock family who lived in a farm on the village's outskirts. On August 3rd a son and daughter died, while the father, John Hancock, died four days later with another son and daughter. Another daughter died on August 9th and the last one the following day, making a total of seven deaths in eight days. The only survivor was Mrs. Hancock. With no one else to help her, she dragged the bodies by hand to a field, dug a separate grave and buried each one. The graveyard still exists today and is known as the Riley Graves. This accomplished, she left the village and went to live with her brother who worked in the cutlery trade in Sheffield.

August also saw grief of another kind, the death of Catherine Mompesson. She had been a comfort to many people and a main stay to her husband during such a time of grief. She died on August 25th, 1666; her tomb can be seen close to the church. Six days after her death, Mompesson finally mustered his courage and wrote to his children about their mother's death:

> *"Dear Hearts*
> *This brings you the doleful news of your dearest mother's death, the greatest*
> *loss that could befall you. I am deprived of a kind and loving consort, and you*
> *are bereaved of the most indulgent mother that ever poor little children had."*

In September the death toll dropped to 24. In the first 11 days of October a further t4 died, but after the IIth the plague stopped abruptly. Out of a total of 350 inhabitants only 83 remained. What a joyful occasion it must have been to the depleted villagers to know that they had survived. Bonfires were lit in the streets and all clothing and bedding burnt, under the supervision of Mompesson who set an example by burning his clothes first.

Here the tale, as far as we are concerned, ends. Eyam settled down to normality and the villagers began to return, although Mompesson left in 1670 and went to Eakring. Eyam had suffered for 13 months in isolation. In gratitude for its self-sacrifice, the village is today visited by thousands each year.

THE PARNASSUS OF THE PEAK

Richard Furness, the Parnassus of the Peak, was born in Eyam on August 2nd, 1791. His life story is a tale of how a country boy, who showed at an early age an aptitude for music, literature and art, became by his own efforts a highly respected and learned man. Through his mother's tuition he could read extremely well by the time he went to school at the age of four. So good in fact was he that Mr. Froggatt, the local surgeon, often came to hear Richard recite from a book. He went to the local village school until he was fourteen years old, and in most of the time that he spent there he was rarely ousted from the top position of the class. He had two particular books that he cherished, Salmon's Geographical Grammar, which he knew by heart, and Don Quixote. The latter he often read while in the house, frequently bursting into laughter.

His parents were farmers and he did his share of the work vigorously, but knowing that his heart lay on the academic side of life. He took pleasure in boasting about the work he had done. At thirteen he mowed an acre of grass in one day by himself—no mean achievement. On another occasion he helped his father to plough a field, but his mind was not on the job and he let the plough wander out of line. His father picked up a grass sod and threw it at him, asking him what the idea was. Awoken from his momentary stupor, he replied: "I was thinking of a rule in Murray's Grammar."

Shortly after leaving school he successfully applied for the post of book-keeper to a couple of firms in Eyam at a salary of £60 per year, but before he could take up the appointment he had to learn the trade of weaving. Two of his uncles persuaded him that there was more money in the practical side of the business and helped to arrange for his apprenticeship to Mr. Joseph Graham, a currier, in Chesterfield. Consequently Richard never became a book-keeper.

Away from home he began laying the foundation stones of his life. He worked long hours, and all his available spare time was taken up by reading. Richard mixed freely with the French soldiers who were on parole in Chesterfield and was soon on very good terms with them, through this relationship he learnt the French language to such an extent that he was capable of reading it fluently. He also began to write poems. One of his earliest he called "My Life," which is about his early childhood and school days. He witnessed a group of villagers at Shirland teasing and provoking a beggar, Richard being so disturbed by their actions that he wrote a poem on their deplorable behaviour. It was pinned to the church door the following Sunday.

When he was seventeen he joined the Wesleyan Methodist church and became a preacher, preaching in the church and in the open. On attaining the age of twenty-one his apprenticeship, which had been most successful, was over. Not having anywhere to go he went to London where, completely out of context with his studious nature, he joined the volunteer army. He was still keen on Methodism and was invited by Dr. Adam Clarke to speak from the pulpit in City Road Chapel, the temple of Methodism. He accepted and his sermon, for one so young, was both moving and stimulating.

Within a year of this success he gave up Methodism. He had returned to Chesterfield and wrote a song to commemorate the defeat of the French in Holland, which was sung to the tune of "God Save the King" at a public dinner held at the Angel Inn. This act shocked the Methodists who told him so afterwards, and as he could not give a reasonable account of his actions he had no option but to leave.

The call of native Derbyshire was too strong and he soon returned to Eyam to set up as a currier. He spent a lot of time courting Francis Ibbotson of Hathersage, whose father was wealthy but was opposed to the match because they were Roman Catholics. However their love was too strong and, in December 1816, they eloped in the middle of the night. The lovers went to the vicar of Hathersage and asked to be married immediately, but this he could not do until after 8 a.m. unless he violated the law. So that no one could get at them he locked Richard and Francis in the church, and minutes after the clock struck eight o'clock they were married. News of the marriage soon reached Francis' father, Matthew, who summoned them to his presence.

"Well, you have fought a hard battle," Francis' father remarked sternly.

"I have won," replied the happy Richard.

This was the beginning of a very happy twenty-eight years of married life. They lived with her father and Richard travelled to Eyam each day to his currier shop. But his "squire's" life at the expensive house of his father-in-law and his assistance given to Mr. Cheetham of Hope, a local doctor, made him neglect his business which soon folded. After four years at Hathersage they had three children, all full of vitality, and it became more abundantly clear to Richard that they had to get away and live on their own. He saw an advertisement for the post of schoolmaster at the free school at Dore, applied and was accepted, and moved to Dore with his family. The school and house were combined and his salary was £18 per annum, but this was later increased to £30. Here he stayed for the rest of his life. In time he became the local registrar and clergy assistant to the church, and his knowledge of medicine, learnt from Mr. Cheetham, made him a most useful member of the village. He wrote a poem on his duties:

I, Richard Furness, schoolmaster, Dore,
Keep parish books and pay the poor;
Draw plans for buildings and indite,
Letters for those who cannot write;
Make wills and recommend a proctor,
Cure wounds, let blood with any doctor;
Draw teeth, sing psalms, the hautboy play
At chapel on each holy day;
Paint sign-boards, cut names at command,
Survey and plot estates of land,
Collect at Easter, one in ten—
And on Sunday, say Amen.

The last line but one, "Collect at Easter, one in ten," refers to the tithes that he collected. Every tenth item was his—the tenth pig of a litter or the tenth part of produce from the land —and was intended for the upkeep of the clergy. The Tithe Commutation Act of 1836 put a stop to this method and henceforth an annual monetary payment was made. However it was not with out its humorous side, as when a woman gave birth to her tenth child and the husband shouted: "Take it to the parson, take it to the parson, it is his tithe."

Richard was extremely busy with his various duties and his family had increased to six children. He drew plans for the modernisation of the church at Dore, which were accepted and carried out under his supervision. His pen had also been busy for he composed many poems, and for thirty years in succession he wrote a hymn for Christmas which he set to music. One poem he wrote to George Stephenson, the railway engineer, on the opening of the North Midland Railway. The last verse was:

His driver's a stoker,
Whose whip is a poker;
And stirs up the corn in his scounce;
Keep out of his line of his push or his kick,
For a giant oak beam is to him but a stick,
He can dash through a wall a hundred feet thick,
And kill you by dozens at once.

Most of his poetic works incorporate some fragments of Derbyshire countryside. For instance, the following are a couple of verses from his poem, *"The Village Boy"*:

Views the amber Derwent's flood
Roll on as far as eye can see;
To him how glorious, Lord of Storms
He wonders what thy seas can be.

Then looks along the mountain tops
Crowned with external blue and gold
Thinks earth a vast extended plain,
Upheld by what? He ne'er was told.

Another was *"Invitation to Matlock Baths"*:

Now the lofty Masson climb,
Through the light and shade sublime . . .
. . . In the distance then behold,
Spire and tunnel glow with gold,
And the Wye, rough Derwent's bridge,
Like a silver serpent glide.

One of his principal poems was *"A Tale of Derwent"* (see chapter on "The Lost Lad"). Two others, *"The Astrologer"* and *"The Rag Bag,"* both contain descriptive passages about the Peakland landscape, especially around Eyam, and are his best works. In 'The Astrologer" the following is part of one of the verses:

Views Win Hill, Mam and Kinderscout.
Below the hills, where the first morning beam,
Pours all its glory on the graves of Eyam,
Where Hollow-brook, in angry winter floods,
Falls, foams and flows down Roylees shelving woods.

"The Rag Bag" was an attack on the dishonesty of the world and is extremely long, but is interwoven with descriptive passages on the Peak:

And Peak's bleak mountains leave it far behind:
Touched by the magnet of the place he loves,
He still veers homeward whereso'er he roves
And joys be more, though barren be the spot.

In 1844 Francis, his wife, died and three years later he retired with a pension of £15 per annum. He moved his large family to a nearby small cottage, and in 1850 he remarried to Mary, the widow of Mr. John Lunn. With their combined income they were able to move into larger premises and lived happily until Richard died on December 13th, 1857. The villagers of Eyam were so proud of Richard that they fetched his body and in a slow candle light procession they crossed the moors back to Eyam. On December 18th he was buried in Eyam churchyard. Just before his death he penned his own *"Requiem"*:   *Farewell, Vain world of noise and show*
Without a lingering look, I view,
Thee, shade of joy, thou real woe,
With all thy charms, adieu, adieu . . .

WILLIAM NEWTON
- MINSTREL OF THE PEAK

The life of this respected gentleman is a success story. From meagre beginnings he built up his knowledge, understanding and ability until he became a prosperous mill owner. Apart from the business side of his life, he had a gift for writing poetry and it is from this outlet that he was soon called the Minstrel of the Peak.

Born at Cockey Farm, near Abney, he was christened William Newton on Christmas Day, 1750. His father was a carpenter, but they were generally poor, and he had only a very brief schooling before going into his father's trade. He quickly picked up the techniques of carpentry, soon becoming highly skilled in the craft, and because his work was good he began amassing a clientele of some of the wealthy people close by. It was while working in their houses that he became acquainted with the world of books. He would browse through them whenever the opportunity arose, this browsing creating an enthusiasm for writing, and especially poetry, which never died.

By the time he was thirty he had married a local girl named Helen Cooke, who came from a similar background to himself. Also, he had begun to collect books and had gathered a small library. The more he read, the more inspired he became to write poetry. His interest in the subject had travelled through the neighbourhood and eventually reached the ears of the Reverend Peter Cunningham, Curate of Eyam and himself a poet. He came to see William and encouraged him to continue writing.

William's greatest friend was Anna Seward, the well known poetess from Lichfield, who encouraged him to pen short verses and poems which were often dedicated to her. She wrote to the Gentleman's Magazine and enclosed the following verse which was published by them soon afterwards.

> *I boast no aid from Phoebus or the nine*
> *No sister graces decorate my line,*
> *The spring Piernan never flowed for me,*
> *Those dulcet waters were reserved for thee.*

A major step in his carpentry work came in 1780 when he was appointed head carpenter for the Duke of Devonshire's building, The Crescent, at Buxton. From then on he began to climb the ladder of success. Six years later he was machinery carpenter at Cressbrook Mill, though not at the building that stands there today, earning a salary of £50 per year. Two years after his appointment the mill and adjacent cottages, one of which was his, were burnt down. It is interesting to note that the old mill had a variety of uses, one being for the manufacture of pepper mint from mint grown in the nearby woods!

With the fire he lost everything and almost his life. His friend, Anna Seward, proved what friendship means at times such as this by raising a few guineas to keep him and his wife going until the bad patch was overcome. She also secured for him the chance of getting a partnership in a new mill to be built on the site of the charred ruins. He needed £200 for his share. Again Anna came forward and gave him £50, £150 coming from the elderly woman he was living with who sold everything she had. Five years after the fire William was worth over £1,000 and before he died he owned Cressbrook Mill. The mill employed over 200 young children in the 1820s who came from orphanages in the south of England. Newton set a precedent in this case, for he did not believe in child brutality nor in keeping them working in poor conditions for long hours. Instead he ensured that they had sufficient rest, good meals, and pleasant working conditions. They even had time to go to Tideswell church on Sundays.

Although he was deeply involved in the mill, he still found time to write poems. His writings, though rarely published yet, were a continual source of interest and pleasure to his friends. Anna Seward wrote: *"The elegance and harmony of Mr. Newton's language, both in prose and verse are miraculous, when it is remembered that till Mr. Cunningham kindly distinguished him, he had only associated with the unlettered and inelegant vulgar."*

In 1797, Newton had the pleasure to listen to and sing a carol he had written. The words were arranged to music by the local musician, Samuel Slack, who resided in Tideswell:

Hymn for Christmas Day, 1797

On the radiant wings of morn
How the Grace Divine are borne,
The spheres celestial ring,
Golden Harps from all the sky
Speak the great Messiah nigh,
And heavenly voices sing "
From man to man let love increase,
To God be Glory and on earth be peace."

Shall not Man, Creation's Lord
To his blissful estate restored,
The mighty chorus raise.
Let him hymn the Great Supreme
Rapture kindles at the theme
And every note is Praise, "
From man to man let love increase,
To God be Glory, and on earth be peace."

Hark, the great Redeemer calls,
Vanquished death before Him falls,
Obedient to His sway;
Comes the High Omniscient Power,
Joyful makes our present hour,
Leads us to endless day.
"From man to man let love increase,
To God be Glory, and on earth be peace."

Although not sung these days, it is certainly a good carol which should be revived and sung in some Peakland church—if only in memory of an able man of yesteryear.

One of his poems relates to gibbeting (see separate section). Newton was so horrified at this use of post and chain that he wrote a poem about the execution of Anthony Lingard of Wardlow. He rarely wrote anything about himself, but the following verse is a brief biography of himself:

Unknown to fame, to Cunningham unknown,
My reed has sounded to the graves alone.
My youth unblest without a friend to cheer.
My hopes to charter or my verse to hear,
I artless tried the Sylvan song to fame;
Spontaneous numbers at my bidding came,
But rugged still unmusical they ran,
And reason blamed what vanity began.

Newton was described by Anna Seward, early in their friend ship: "This self taught bard is rather handsome, but aims at nothing in his appearance but the clean and decent." It was Anna, too, who wrote the final note about him in the Sheffield Iris in 1830 shortly after his death:

"He died as he had lived, in peace and charity with all men, beloved and mourned by his family and respected and regretted by his friends."

The gravestone to William Newton can be seen in the graveyard of Tideswell church, and is headed *"The Minstrel of The Peak."*

A RENOWNED VOCALIST
—SAMUEL SLACK

DERBYSHIRE has produced many interesting and likable characters. Samuel Slack, born in Tideswell in 1737, rose to national fame but retained his native approach to life. He first became known when he applied for a job in a college choir at Cambridge. The applicants all sat in one room and heard each other perform. When it was Samuel's turn he sang Purcell's famous air, *"They that go down to the sea in ships."* After he had finished the choirmaster said to the other applicants, *"Gentle men, I now leave it with you whether anyone will sing after what you have just heard."* They all left.

From then on he never looked back. Georgiana, Duchess of Devonshire, took a particular interest in Samuel's singing ability and arranged to have Mr. Spofforth, the best singing master in England at that time, to tutor him at her expense. One writer at this period wrote:

> *Slack, when first he struck the town,*
> *Possess'd no slender musical renown;*
> *Science his early song with meaning grac'd,*
> *And practice soon improved his native taste.*

Spofforth soon realised that he had a person of unusual ability and gift for music. Within a very short time he had improved beyond recognition and went to London where he sang the bass part at many festivals, thrilling and astounding the audiences with his powerful voice. Following a show he kept himself to himself and did not mingle with the other singers This caused a writer to pen: *"He was addicted to some of the low tastes of the day and also an inveterate lover of the pot and pipe. He did not possess much delicacy in the choice of his company, nor was he very elegant in his conversation."*

On one occasion he became so intoxicated that after leaving the pub he found a field close by where he curled up on the grass to sleep it off. A few hours later a bull came up to his slumbering body and turned it over. Samuel looked up, bewildered, and saw the huge face of the bull close to his. He let out a whole paragraph of abuse in his loudest and deepest voice at the bull which stared and ran away terrified!

A highlight in his career was when he was summoned to sing before King George the third. After the recital, one of the king's servants came to him and expressed his majesty's message of enjoyment at his singing. "Oh," said Slack, "he wer pleased, wer he? Ah, I know'd I could dow't."

On another occasion he was singing at the George Hotel in Tideswell where his wife had arranged to meet him. When she left their house in Litton she could hear Samuel's voice from over a mile away. When he retired he returned to live in Tides well, regularly attending the meetings of the *"Catch and Gee Club."* He was a popular member and would often sing a few songs for them, especially his favourite *"Life's a bumper, filled by fate."* *"Life's a bumper"* came to be the title of a painting by Potts of Slack and six others merrily singing with glasses in their hands.

At the age of 65 he passed away quietly in August 1822, but it was not until 1831 that a gravestone was placed to his memory:

> *"This stone was erected by the voluntary contributions of the Barlow Choir and a few other admirers of that noble deep-toned melodist."*

Towards the end of the nineteenth century the memorial was in ruins, and an appeal was launched in the Sheffield Weekly Independent to restore it. This was done and the memorial to Samuel Slack remains with us today in Tideswell graveyard close to that of the *"Minstrel of the Peak."*

THE ASHFORD DWARF

Derbyshire has "owned" every conceivable type of person from eccentric characters to learned scholars. Molly Bray must surely rate as one of the most unusual. Born in the 1720s, she never grew any taller than three feet.

She lived in a cottage opposite the southern front of the church at Ashford-in-the-Water. Of her early life—her parents, schooling or jobs—we know nothing except that she was very beautiful. Molly was well liked by the village and neighbourhood and was affectionately nicknamed *"Owd Molly Bree."* She never hurt anyone nor stole anything, her only fault being cleanliness, or the lack of it. No one was ever allowed into her cottage until she died, when the inside was a sorrowful sight of squalor.

Molly walked around the village slowly, being spoken to by all who passed by. Often she went into other people's houses, especially during the winter months to warm herself, and when she left the owners would discreetly sweep the area where she had been sitting. Her favourite occupation was taking trips to the neighbouring villages especially to Bakewell. On these occasions she wore *"a wide-awake hat, an old scarlet cloak or loose bed-gown, a thin handkerchief around her head and chin, and a breasted pinafore—both cloak and pinafore being extremely ragged and jagged at the ends."* To complete her appearance she carried a basket on one arm and held a knob stick in the other hand. She looked an unusual sight, for when standing up her feet turned in at an angle of 45 degrees. En route to a village, as soon as a coach came along she would immediately squat on the road and tuck her legs under her body. Invariably the passengers would throw her a copper or two before proceeding.

This is all we know about Molly, except the entry in the Ashford church register which says, *"Buried, March 11th, 1811, Mar Bray."* She died in her cottage and was believed to be about 85 years old. The reason for her surviving so long is, as one nineteenth century writer, noted: *"Like many long-livers, she indulged somewhat immoderately in the narcotic weed."*

THE BAKEWELL RIOTS

The Bakewell Riots took place in 1796-97 and were the result of the Militia Ballot Act. The High Peak was supposed to contribute one hundred men towards the county's total of 560. Rumour had spread around that Derbyshire was supplying more people than any other county and from this reason, which was only based on hearsay, stemmed the demonstrations.

Each county had a lieutenant, who was responsible for the selection of persons, usually by ballot, to serve in the Militia. In Derbyshire's case the Dukes of Devonshire had been the lieutenants. To help him in his work he had several deputies, who had to be approved by the sovereign prior to engagement. The deputies were capable of assuming full control if the lieutenant was away.

The Militia was a three year contract, and anyone between the ages of 18 and 50 was eligible. It generally met about four times a year for training, unless there was a war. Every man who earned £500 or over a year, or had £6,000 in goods or money, was liable to purchase a horse, horseman and arms. Every man having a yearly wage of £50, or who had £600 in goods or money, was liable to pay for a foot soldier. Although paid for individually, the state paid when the people were engaged in battle. It was permissible for a person who had been elected to the Militia to send a substitute for training or even war, although naturally this was at his own expense. Should a county not supply its quota of men the county authority was fined. Having been balloted, one received the following document:

> *"This is to certify that ....was drawn by lot at Chesterfield, to serve in the Militia, for the County of Derbyshire date.."*

This system of balloting continued for many years, but after 1852 voluntary enlistment became predominant.

The first demonstration was a very mild affair, and one which no one took very seriously. On market day a group of forty people marched into Bakewell armed with clubs and spades. The waitress of the White Horse Inn saw them coming, ran into the dining-room and shouted, *"The mob is coming—the mob!"* The occupants remained unmoved and continued eating for they "thought proper that no one should notice the mob." At the town hall the mob made speeches and threatened to come again when the magistrates were in town. In an orderly manner they retired to the White Horse Inn, drank a pint of ale which they paid for and then dispersed.

No one took their threat seriously and when the magistrates came they marched again, but in bigger numbers. The mob forced their way into the room where the magistrates were holding their court. Startled at this intrusion, the magistrates sat there while the mob collected all the ballot papers. They searched the magistrates' pockets and even the chairman's, and then burnt the papers in front of the White Horse Inn. The inhabitants of Bakewell were disgusted at their actions and many volunteered to be sworn in as special constables, although the offer was not accepted

The next time the magistrates came they brought with them a detachment of cavalry. Again an even bigger mob came, some from Castleton, Baslow, Longstone and Eyam, but was soon scattered by the cavalry who took six prisoners. These prisoners all came from Baslow and were not inhabitants of Bakewell; the following day they were remove(l and sent to Chesterfield jail. The cost of suppressing this riot came to £161-19s.-7d. (£161.97p.), the two most expensive items being:

236 dinners at 1/3 each £14-15s.-10d. (£14.79p)

Wine £12-16s.-6d. (£12.82p)

The cost for the six prisoners was "Eating and ale—6s. 0d. (30p)"

The cavalry soon left and the Roxburgh Fencibles came and lived in the town and neighbourhood to maintain the peace. They were not needed, for peace reigned and after several months they left. There were similar demonstrations at this time for the same reasons at Ashbourne and Wirksworth, but these were only mild affairs in contrast to Bakewell's. The only thing that the riots did was to remove the Epiphany Quarter Sessions which had been held in Bakewell, to Derby. In 1800 Bakewell issued a petition with numerous signatures to try and restore the sessions to the town but it came to nothing.

THE BAKEWELL WITCHES

King James 1st was a very superstitious man and during his reign over 3,000 witches were hung. Two of them came from Bakewell and were executed in 1608 at Derby. The tale of how they were discovered and sentenced to death reveals a clever plan by a man who wanted to take his revenge.

Mrs. Stafford and her sister, the "supposed witches," were milliners in Bakewell. They also ran a lodging house which was popular and always in demand. One day a Scotsman, having inquired where he could stay, was directed to Mrs. Stafford's residence and remained for a few days before being asked for some money. He replied that he hadn't any, so Mrs. Stafford took some of his clothes as payment and turned him out. He felt extremely sore at her action but continued on his way, eventually reaching London. As he had no money and was inadequately clothed, he found an unused cellar to sleep in. In the early morning a night watchman, who thought he was planning some mischievous adventure, found him and quickly escorted him to the nearest magistrate. Knowing he was in a tight spot and wanting revenge on Mrs. Stafford and the witch-ridden state of the country, he fabricated the following story to the magistrate:

He said the previous day he had been at Mrs. Stafford's house in Bakewell. After going to bed, he woke up for some unknown reason at 3 a.m. and could see a small ray of light coming from a chink in the floorboards. Inquisitiveness got the better of him and he crept from the bed and peered through the crack—below he could see Mrs. Stafford and her sister preparing to go out. He lingered a while and watched their movements, before he heard Mrs. Stafford say:

"Over thick, over thin,
Now, Devil, to the cellar in Lunnon."

As soon as she had said the last word the light went out and they disappeared.

Mystified, the Scotsman returned to his bed, thoughtful. He could not get to sleep again, for his mind kept pondering about the recent events. While thinking he mumbled the rhyme to himself. Immediately the bed clothes fell to the floor and a gush of air carried him through space to beside Mrs. Stafford in the cellar in London. They did not seem to notice him, and he watched them tying up parcels of cloth. Shortly, Mrs. Stafford gave him a drink, which he drank quickly. Instantly he fell asleep and the next thing he knew was the night watchman in the cellar.

The magistrate, sensing witchcraft, fell for the tale and issued orders that the Scotsman be freed and given some clothes. He also authorised a warrant for the arrest of Mrs. Stafford and her sister for witchcraft. The police went to their house and found the clothes belonging to the Scotsman, confirming his story and their fate. The Scotsman was avenged and, despite the pleas of innocence, the two Bakewell witches were hung.

MARTHA TAYLOR
—THE FASTING DAMSEL

An eye-witness who saw Martha in 1669, when she had been fasting for about nine months, wrote the following: "Her pulse pretty smooth even and lively in its motions, seldom diverted out of usual course, but when she was under some immediate sorry of mind or body. Her eyes, though often weak, were some times quick and durable in their beholding or dwelling upon subjects, so that she would know that she looked upon at the first glance, and continue reading for an hour or more together." He also took notice of her general appearance: her face was plump and had a fair complexion, but the rest of her body was like a skeleton.

There is no gimmick about the above, which is authentic. Martha fasted for over a year, not for a publicity stunt, but because she could not bring herself to eat. To ascertain that there was nothing deceptive in her fast, which had become of national interest, the neighbouring villages selected between 40 and 60 women. Working on a rota system, two of them were in Martha's room all the time keeping watch. The Earl of Devonshire had a group of investigators watch and interview everyone who came, but they likewise could find no fault or anything suspicious.

Martha Taylor was born in Over Haddon, near Bakewell, in February 1651. Her parents were simple but honest folk and her father worked as a lead miner. For the first ten years of Martha's life she ate well, went to school and played outside—in other words she lived a perfectly normal life. At ten years of age the next door neighbour accidentally hit her in the back; there is no evidence to assume that this was a premeditated action, but this blow was gravely to affect her life. Soon afterwards paralysis set in and she was confined to bed. For the next year she ate normally, but was unable to get out of bed unaided. Then for a brief period in May 1662 her paralysis subsided and she ventured downstairs a couple of times before it returned permanently. The next five years were uneventful—although a confined existence, she made the best of it by reading and taking an interest in life generally.

In September 1667, and for the next four months, her body went through every conceivable pain and convulsion. Tears of blood ran down her face and she was perpetually being sick, often violently. She ate very little and what she did eat was soon brought back. A couple of months later she began to hiccup loudly, often being heard several doors away Cramp followed next and by December her weakened body looked as though it was ready to utter the last sigh. With death on the doorstep, Martha first lost the use of her voice and shortly after fell unconscious. In this state she remained for two weeks. She regained consciousness first and then her speech returned, although she still continued to vomit. It was at this time that she began to show a dislike for feed Although each day she regained more of her usual self, she had no desire to eat anything. Every day her parents brought what they hoped would be attractive food to her, but nothing would induce Martha to eat. In the end, her parents realised the futility of food-bearing and ceased doing so, only taking some up on request.

As the weeks slipped by, word of these unusual circumstances filtered through the area until it became of national interest. Many learned people from London, physicians, scholars and professors, came to see and investigate this unusual phenomenon. John Gratton, the Quaker Apostle of the Peak, often came and wrote in his journal: "*But sometimes I went two miles to see a woman at Over Haddon, who pretended to live without meat; where I met with professors (I think I may say) of all sorts.*"

During this fast many things happened to her. She once went without sleep for five weeks, another time she temporarily went deaf. If anyone put flowers in her room, Martha would say they were too strong for her brain! The only nourishment Martha had, which was at infrequent intervals, was the odd raisin. On rare occasions she asked for a drink, such as wine or milk, to moisten her lips. The only time she ate anything of any size was a fig. Having eaten it, Martha was violently sick for the next 24 hours and it took a long time for her body to quieten down. To keep the public informed of the latest developments, three writers were so moved by what they saw that four pamphlets about her and their observations were published:

1. "*News from Derbyshire or the Wonder of Wonders that has ever been printed.*" By T. Robins, and published in October 1668.

2. "*The Wonder of the World'*—the book is taken from Martha's lips and her mother's. By T. Robins.

3. "*The famous Derbyshire Damsel; proving that without any miracle, the texture of human bodies may be so altered that life may long be continued without the supplies of meat and drink; with an account of the heart and how far it is interested in the business of fermentation.*" By Joseph Reynolds.

4. "*Mirabile Pecci or the non-such Wonder of the Peak. Preservation of Martha Taylor, one that hath been supported in time above a year, beyond the ordinary course of nature, without meat or drink.*"

Although her parents were now famous, they took no heed of it and carried on their normal lives as much as possible. Alas, as to what happened after a year's fast we do not know. There is no evidence to reconstruct what took place. We are left to wonder —did she continue fasting or did she eat and walk about? The only concrete piece of evidence we have is in the Bakewell Parish Register, where her burial is entered on June 12th, 1684. If correct, she lived a further fifteen years.

THE KING OF THE PEAK

Haddon Hall, near Bakewell, is the finest surviving example of a manorial home in England. It is fitting, therefore, that one of its owners, Sir George Vernon, should be locally called the King of the Peak. Sir George inherited the estate when he was nine years old in 1517 and, as it turned out, he was the last male Vernon to own the Hall. He earned his title, as Stephen Glover wrote in 1830, "*on account of his almost royal style of living; his retinue was numerous and his behaviour, as well as his hospitality, was magnificent and princely.*" Another wrote: "It is said that he was one of the most generous and hospitable, as well as just and strict men, although given perhaps to undue severity and to an indulgence in '*Lynch Law*' and that he lived and died in the 'good esteem' of most men."

It was his indulgence in the "*Lynch Law*" which gave rise to the most colourful event of his life. The tale runs thus A pedlar, who often visited Derbyshire, was in the neighbourhood of Haddon Hall selling his wares. Soon afterwards he was found murdered; the last time he had been seen was when he entered a cottage. Sir George sent for the body and had it placed in the hall of Haddon and covered with a sheet. This accomplished, he summoned the cottager and questioned him as to the fate of the pedlar but he denied knowing anything. Sir George then gathered several servants and the cottager together and went into the hall, where he uncovered the body and asked everyone present to come in turn to touch it. "*The ordeal by touch,*" as it was called, was a means of finding out the murderer. The guilty person, when he touched the body, "*will shed forth blood.*" When the cottager's turn came he fled, so immediately Sir George ordered his men to catch and hang him. They finally caught him at Ashford-in-the-Water, where he was hanged in a field which was for many years known as Gallows Acre.

But this is not the end of the tale. Sir George's unusual action of hanging a man without trial meant he had to go to London to face charges. In the court he was twice summoned as "*The King of the Peak,*" to which he gave no reply. On the third summons he was called Sir George Vernon, when he stepped forward and said "Here am I!" Since the indictment was in the name of "*The King of the Peak*" the case was dismissed and he was discharged.

Sir George married twice. His first wife, Margaret, daughter of Sir Gilbert Talboy, gave birth to two girls, christened Margaret and Dorothy. His second wife, Maude, daughter of Sir Ralph Longford, gave birth to several males, but none survived infancy. When Sir George died in 1567 he left his estates, which numbered over thirty by this time, to be equally divided between his daughters Margaret and Dorothy. Dorothy and her husband, John Manners, son of the Earl of Rutland, inherited Haddon. From this period onwards to the present day the Dukes of Rutland have owned this Hall.

This section would be incomplete if it did not mention the courtship of Dorothy and John. Sir George did not approve of this relationship, although he later became reconciled to their marriage shortly before his death. Their love life had therefore to be carried out in secret to avoid his wrath. Their final meeting was on the occasion of the marriage of Margaret, Dorothy's sister, when a ball was held in Haddon Hall. When the clock chimed midnight Dorothy slipped out and into the nearby woods and there met her lover who was dressed as a forester. Together they rode to Leicester and were married at Aylestone.

The tombs of Sir George Vernon, Dorothy Vernon and Sir John Manners can be seen in the Vernon Chapel at Bakewell church.

SIR CHRISTOPHER FULWOOD - A ROYALIST

In Bradford Dale, just east of Middleton, is a small rock cave in between two boulders close to the path to Hopping Farm. It is known as Fulwood's Cave, or Cromwell's Cave, although both names are rarely used these days. However, there is an interesting though sad tale as to how it acquired its name.

In the sixteenth century Sir George Fulwood, who was a lawyer by profession, built a large embattled house at Middleton, near Youlgreave. The house was called Fulwood's Castle, the money for it coming from a lead mine known as Fulwood Pipe which proved to he an exceedingly rich vein. Christopher Fulwood, born in London in 1590, was the eldest son and heir to Sir George. Christopher went into law and worked at Grays Inn in London; in 1626 he was Autumn Reader and became treasurer in 1637.

Upon his father's death in 1624 Christopher inherited the house at Middleton, meaning he had to make his base in Derbyshire. For the next twenty years he earned a respected name and became a fair judge. Christopher was a keen royalist, and he did not hesitate to gather men to serve the cause of Charles 1st. The following note is taken from a letter to Charles 1st in the Harlech Collection at the British Museum. *"The breaking out of the civil war, he adhered to the King's interest with great zeal and was employed to raise the Derbyshire miners as a Life-guard for his Majesty, when the Lord Lieutenant of the County, the Earl of Rutland, refused to appear with the service."*

Christopher indeed set about with enthusiasm and vigour, for in a short time he had gathered a regiment of over 1,100 men on Tideswell Moor. The gathering of so large a group of supporters considerably alarmed the parliamentary leaders. Christopher was now a wanted man and Sir John Gell, the parliamentary Governor of Derbyshire, sent a selected band to capture him. Before they reached Fulwood's Castle he slipped out and ran down into Brad ford Dale, hut unfortunately he had been seen. He found the small cave and hid inside where he was shot and wounded by the parliamentarians. Removing his body, they set off for Lichfield which Sir John Gell had only just captured. Sir Christopher died on the journey at Calton, in Staffordshire, on November 6th 1643.

Fulwood's Castle fell into ruin and was dismantled in the seventeenth century, the stone being used for constructing farm buildings and the nearby Castle Farm. Today you can still see a rough outline of where the house once stood, a wall and the drive.

THE BATTLE OF HARTINGTON MOOR

Hartington Moor (Grid Ref. 145617) has been a battle ground on two occasions, the first being in 80 A.D. when the British tribes tried to stop the advancing Roman army. The second was in 1651, when the principal figure was William de Rossington. There is no tombstone to him, but gravestones and tombs to other members of the family can be seen in Youlgreave and Ashbourne churches. The one at Youlgreave, in the chancel, is to Sir John Rossington who lies cross-legged with a heart in his hand. According to legend, a huntsman chased his prey into the church, thus committing sacrilege, and for punishment his heart is supposed to have leapt out into his hand.

William de Rossington was a soldier and served in King Charles the first's army. His brother lived with their sister at home in Rowsley, managing the estate. William proved himself to be a good soldier, full of courage and a clever horseman, but his brother died unexpectedly leaving him no option but to resign his commission and retire to Rowsley and look after the estate. William was a royalist at heart. When King Charles the second planned to come down from Scotland and collect his faithful supporters en route, William naturally offered his services and planned to gather a small regiment. He was decidedly against Parliament and Cromwell, and was eager to see the monarchy restored. From the neighbouring villages, William enlisted four hundred men and, using a field by his house, he drilled the men each morning to teach them the art of fighting. Most of the men were farmers or miners and were unfamiliar with weapons. Before they were fully fighting fit, William learnt that the royalist army planned to arrive at Wigan under the leadership of the Earl of Newcastle on August 20th, 1651. William planned to meet them there.

William was single but was deeply in love with Anna, daughter of the squire who lived at Holme Hall in Bakewell. They met regularly and the last night before he departed was no exception. They sat entwined in their love, putting off their farewells. Although Anna was happy but sad at his impending departure, William felt that she appeared to have something on her mind. Her discomfort was a vivid dream that she had the night before the dream concerning them both. While walking through a wood together, Cromwell and a few supporters suddenly surrounded them from behind a tree. Taking William away, they manhandled him to the nearest suitable tree and at Cromwell's orders began preparing to hang him. Before they had time to fit a noose around his neck, Anna shrieked and woke up.

Having retold her dream, Anna was in an emotional state. However consoling William was, nothing would persuade Anna to forget her dream, but time did not stand still and they had to part. William's final words were: *"Anna, my love, banish from thy mind such baseless freaks of troubled fancy, now I must away, tomorrow comes apace, one kiss and away to Hartington. Adieu my love, my Anna."* Anna watched him go, not knowing that this would be the last time she would see him alive.

The scene at Rowsley the next day was never forgotten by the villagers. Four hundred men gathered ready to leave, their wives and loved ones clinging to their necks. It was approaching midday before William led the men out, at Hartington they were joined by further royalists from the High Peak, increasing their numbers to over six hundred. Being late in the day, they camped on Hartington Moor. Meanwhile, parliamentary scouts had been observing William's movements and reported back to Sir John Gell, the parliamentary governor of Derby. He issued orders that William should be intercepted and next day, as they began preparing to depart, William saw to his horror a large group of men approaching him. Colonel Lilburn had been directed from York to break up this royalist army. William quickly assembled his men ready for the forthcoming onslaught, and in no time at all they were all engaged in deadly combat. For many hours each side advanced a few feet before being repulsed. Although William's men were barely trained they fought courageously, their leader being an inspiration to them all. He stood at the front with sword in hand and battled away impervious to the blows he received, but by late afternoon the parliamentary army was slowly imposing its superiority. Suddenly William collapsed and died from the numerous wounds he had received. The whole of William's army dispersed—their leader was dead and nothing would induce them to fight on.

Early in the evening Anna learnt the fate of her lover. Although filled with grief, she knew she must locate his body and bury it. She had also heard that Lingard had issued a reward for William, dead or alive, for they did not see him fall. Lingard had a sinister plan to place William's head on a pole and exhibit it in Rowsley. Anna mounted her horse and with four close friends sped away to the battleground. In darkness they crept through the lifeless bodies, turning them over and searching for William. At last they found his bloodstained body, fastened him to the spare horse and quickly left. Their destination was Hedburn Wood, near Cressbrook, about ten miles away. Beside the wood these five mournful figures dug a shallow grave, the four standing back to let Anna place her dear one into the grave. For a while she hugged and kissed his body before she summoned up sufficient courage to release it. The grave was filled in and the five rode away, never to mention what they had done.

There the tale ends, but over two hundred years later a farmer called Hoff was digging a hole for a gatepost. Suddenly he heard the scraping of metal and in a little while he uncovered a helmet, sword, buttons and a few bones which unmistakably were William de Rossington's. For a few months it became a place to visit to see this simple grave to a bold soldier. In recent times, while ploughing on Hartington Moor, lead bullets have been uncovered bearing the letter "P" for Parliament or Protector.

CHARLES COTTON
—LAUREATE OF THE DOVE

CHARLES COTTON and his faithful friend, Izaak Walton, the two renowned fishermen, are synonymous with the river Dove. It inspired Cotton to write verse, of which the following three lines are perhaps his most famous:

O my beloved Nymph, fair Dove!
Princess of rivers! How I love
Upon thy flowery banks to lie!

He was born within sight of the Dove at Beresford Hall on April 28th, 1630. For the whole of his life he rarely left the place, always preferring his friends to come to him rather than he to them. Cotton had no normal education, instead, he was encouraged by his father to read the many books in his library. He soon acquired a liking for poetry, and his father had many poetical acquaintances, which increased his interest.

On June 30th, 1656, he married Isabella Hutchinson at St. Mary's Church, Nottingham. They produced a large family but only one son and four daughters survived infancy. When his father died in 1658 Cotton inherited the estate. His father was an extravagant man, and the financial side of the estate was extremely unhealthy. Charles likewise was extravagant, and the problem of money, with creditors continually calling at the Hall, proved to be his biggest worry. Often he would slip out of the Hall and hide in a cave in Beresford Dale, only to creep out again when the creditor had left!

Cotton was a confirmed royalist although he did not take part in any of the conflicts. Shortly after the restoration of the monarchy in 1660 he became a revenue commissionaire for the counties of Derbyshire and Staffordshire. In 1665 he was appointed a magistrate, and furthered his career in 1667 when he was given a Captain's commission in Lord Chesterfield's regiment. His wife, Isabella, died in 1669 and the following year Cotton went to Ireland to serve under the Duke of Ormonde. Unfortunately, the Duke was removed from his post and Cotton's trip came to nothing. Four years later, in 1674, Cotton married again, his bride being the Dowager Countess of Ardglass. She had a considerable estate but this did not solve his financial position. He applied to Parliament for permission to sell some land which was held by trustees, his debts amounting to over £8,000.

However, at this time he had a fishing house built in Beresford Dale close to the Dove and, although it stands on private land today, it remains his eternal monument. Over the doorway are his initials and Izaak Walton's, cleverly entwined. It is not known the precise date when these two fishermen met, but Izaak Walton married for the second time in 1646 to the daughter of a Bishop who had a cottage in Dovedale so their first meeting must have been shortly afterwards. Cotton would sit beside the fishing house and smoke his pipe which he said was *"always my breakfast "* He wrote about the Dove with joy, and perhaps penned the following lines beside the house:

> *Men fall in love*
> *With thy bright beauties and thy fairest eyes.*
> *Would like a Parthian whilst the shorter flies.*
> *Of all fair Thetis daughters none so bright,*
> *So pleasant none to taste, none to the sight,*
> *None yields the gentle Angler such delight.*

Izaak Walton wrote The Compleat Angler, the first edition coming out in 1653. Cotton wrote a second section for the book on Derbyshire, which appeared in the fifth edition published in 1676. The book is subtitled *"The Contemplative Man's Recreation, being a discourse of Fish and Fishing not unworthy the perusal of most anglers."* It is still revered by many fishermen.

Cotton wrote another book *Wonders of the Peak,* which came out in 1681 and was dedicated to the Duchess of Devonshire. In it he lists and extols the beauties of the seven wonders of the Peak District—Pooles Hole; St. Ann's Well, Buxton; Tideswell; Eldon Hole; Mam Tor; Peak Cavern; and Chatsworth.

Pooles Hole (Grid Ref. 046726) near Buxton, is named after an outlaw called Poole who kept his spoils in the cavern. Having explored its inner depths, Cotton continues: *"And you shall see the cheerful day again; when after two hours' darkness you will say the sun appears deft, in a brighter ray. Thus after long restraint, when once set free, men better taste the 'Air of Liberty'."*

Six hundred paces away is the second "wonder"—St. Ann's Well. The third wonder is another well, this time at Tideswell:

> *This fountain is so very very small,*
> *The observer hardly can perceive it crawl.*

Cotton came eleven times to see some movement in the stream, and it was only on his last visit that he could detect any!

Eldon Hole (Grid Ref. 116809), near Peak Forest, was the fourth wonder and one which captured his imagination to the full. He tried to measure its depth and calculated this to be 884 yards deep—it is in fact only 180 feet!

> But when I peep into it, I must declare,
> My heart still beats and eyes with horror stare
> And he, that standing on the brink of Hell,
> Can carry it so unconcerned, and well,
> As to betray no Fear, is certainly
> A better Christian: or worse than I.

Next is Mam Tor (Grid Ref. 128835)

> Enough of Hell! From whence you forward ride;
> Still mounting up the Mountains growing side,
> Till having gained the utmost height,
> you eye Northward a mile, Mam Tor.

Contained in the description of this wonder is the story of a wager, when a local was dared to climb the crumbling southern face. This face has given rise to the name, Shivering Mountain:

> That hands and feet were ready hold to quit,
> And to the fool their master's fate submit.
> How to advance a step he could not tell,
> And to descend was as impossible.
> For to the spectators' wonder, and his own,
> He panting gained at last the mountain crown.

The sixth wonder was Peak Cavern in Castleton:

> Under this castle yawns a dreadful cave,
> Whose light may well astonish the most brave,
> And make him pause, ere further he proceed
> T'explore what in those gloomy vaults lie hid.

The seventh and last wonder is Chatsworth (Grid Ref. 263703):

> There stands a stately and stupendous pile.

In 1681 Cotton's financial position was hopeless and he had no alternative but to sell Beresford Hall. Fortunately, his cousin, John Beresford of Newton Grange, four miles from Ashbourne, purchased the Hall and allowed Charles to live there until he died in 1687.

Cotton was buried at St. James', Piccadilly. The Hall was pulled down in 1856, but this "old fashioned country squire," as he called himself. has left us with a wealth of poems for eternity.

PHOEBE BROWN
—A CELEBRITY OF MATLOCK

A nineteenth century writer said of Phoebe Brown: *"She was rough, rude, uncouth, eccentric, masculine, but she knew what was right and in her rough way, abided by it."* Born in 1770, her parents were working class, which meant Phoebe had very little education at all. At an early age she began to appreciate literature and would read avidly the works of Milton, Shakespeare and Pope. Often, in later life, she would quote a long passage from one of the writers. She lived with her mother in a tiny cottage opposite the huge rock bastion of High Tor, and when her mother died she inherited the cottage. She sought fame, but none of her talents led her to stardom except her eccentric character. Phoebe became extremely well known, and any traveller who came to Matlock rarely failed to have a look at this unusual woman.

One of Phoebe's oddities was to dress in men's clothes. Invariably she would parade around wearing a man's woollen coat, a petticoat, several handkerchiefs on her head tied under her chin, and a man's hat on top. Her outward appearance was therefore decidedly male. To further enact this male streak she had some surprisingly masculine abilities. She was adept in masonry and carpentry, she could mow and reap and could work as an hostelier, farrier, groom and horse breaker. Horse breaking for ladies proved a lucrative sideline, for she charged a guinea a week for this service. Phoebe was also one of the best judges of racehorses in the country, and many people would not place their bets until they heard her comments.

Music was her greatest love and the flute became her favourite companion. A visitor came one day and picked up the flute and played a little tune, but Phoebe took it from him saying she could play better The only comment about the sound which emitted was that it was rather loud! Her musical knowledge was gained from a travelling harpist—she was given a harpsichord, although she could not play it, and she built an extra room on to the house to keep it in. Phoebe also played the violin and the 'cello, and was for many years the leader of the Matlock Church Choir.

Although she remained single, she liked attention and being fussed over. She was an extremist in every sense of the word. If she liked people, Phoebe would tell everyone so and would give them individual attention which often proved embarrassing. On the other hand, if she disliked them, they were well advised to keep out of her way. Every time she spotted them, Phoebe would not miss an opportunity to be rude or make fun of them. Her food mainly consisted of consuming large quantities of milk, she ate no beef or pork, but a little mutton, and never drank wine, ale or spirits.

On one occasion a visitor came from Liverpool and during their conversation she suggested to Phoebe that she should come and visit her. Naturally, she did not expect Phoebe to come, but a few months later there was a knock on the door Phoebe had taken up the invitation and arrived on horseback in the middle of winter. The host was stunned to see Phoebe, but did her utmost to make her at home. When Phoebe left she insisted, although there was snow on the ground, on walking to Matlock. Phoebe was a good walker and could average between thirty and forty miles a day— she is reported to have done fifty miles on one occasion.

Another of her eccentric characteristics was her fear of being robbed. Her house was like a miniature arsenal. Most of the time she carried a rifle on her shoulder and, to her credit, she was a notable markswoman. Neatly stacked in the corners of the living room were guns and spears, many of which she fabricated herself by creating razor sharp edges. As she grew old her circle of friends and guests diminished, much to her sadness for it also meant a drop in money, which had frequently been given by her callers. In the end she became penniless. Just before she began to beg the Duke of Devonshire stepped in and gave her an allowance of 5s.(25P) per week until she died. At her request the curate of Mat lock, the Reverend Gaunt, wrote her epitaph, which runs thus:

> Here lies romantic Phoebe,
> Half Garymede, half Hebei;
> A maid of notable condition,
> Jockey, cow herd and musician.

She died in May 1854, at the age of 84.

JEDEDIAH BUXTON
—ARITHMETICAL GENIUS
OF THE PEAK

DERBYSHIRE has produced many fascinating and unusual people, but Jedediah must rate as the most outstanding. He was born on March 20th, 1707, at Elmton, nine miles east of Chesterfield, near Cresswell; his father was schoolmaster of the village, and his grandfather, the vicar. Despite his next of kin being learned men, Jedediah never went to school nor had any formal education. Even at the time of his death he was unable to read or write the English language. The only book which he did read and master to a phenomenal degree was a table of multiplication. It was this incredible capacity for calculation which brought him from obscurity to being not only a wonder of Derbyshire but of England.

He generally worked as a labourer on a nearby farm, but often helped surveyors when they were measuring a field or house. Sir John Rodes, who lived at Elmton, wanted to know the size of his land. Jedediah walked round the property and gave him the figures in acres, rods, perches and, for interest, in square inches, and then for amusement worked out the total area in square hair breadths. All this was done without the use of pen or paper. When a team of surveyors later accurately measured the grounds, Jedediah's figures were found to be only an inch out!

During the years 1751-1754 many of his calculations appeared in the Gentleman's Magazine. In 1754 he walked to London, principally to see the king, who unfortunately was away so he could not achieve his ambition. However he visited the Royal Society and gave a demonstration of his remarkable calculating ability. They put a question to him, and calculating in his head, he answered them. For example: "A field 423 yards long by 383 yards wide, what is the area?" Within two minutes he replied "162,009 yards." The correct answer.

"How many acres does the above field measure?" Jedediah took eleven minutes to answer, but was eventually right—33 acres, 1 rod, 35 perch and 20 1/4 yards.

"How many barley corns would reach eight miles?" Taking a minute and a half for the calculation, he replied, "1,520,640 barley corns."

His finest calculation was the day of his death! He worked for the Duke of Portland and one day he told the butler he urgently wanted to see the Duke. The butler ushered him in and the Duke asked what all the urgency was about.

"I am come to thank your Grace for all the favours you have bestowed on me, for I shall never see your Grace anymore."

"What makes you so sure you won't?" replied the Duke.

"I must never see you again; I must come here no more."

"Why, Jeddy?" replied the Duke.

"Because I shall die on Thursday next."

The Duke told him he was talking rubbish and informed the servants not to give him any beer, *"for the old man's brain goes weak."* Over the next few days Jedediah bade farewell to his friends, but they all laughed at him and thought it was a joke. The day dawned and after dinner he sat in a chair and to every one's amazement, died. The date was March 5th, 1772.

BELPER JOE

Joe,s biography is well summed up by a writer who wrote the following, about eighty years ago: *"Born a beggar, brought up as a beggar, lived a beggar's life, and died a pauper's death in the workhouse."*

Although Joe Houghton was born in Derby, he spent the greater part of his life in Belper where he earned the nickname "Belper Joe." He was primarily a beggar, but he occasionally did do some work to earn a few coppers. He was a shy man, and if left alone he would not interfere with people or swear at them. However, if teased he came out of his shell and would hurl abuse in retaliation. Few people cared for him, but could always spot him coming down the street by his dress. His trousers were baggy and tied at the waist by a piece of rope, and his overcoat was invariably elbowless and reached well down his legs. But the most unmistakable object was his tall black hat, the rim of which had long given up the idea of being rigid!

Belper Joe was his popular nickname, but he also had a curious habit of touching objects and people while he walked the streets. This habit earned him another nickname—Touch. Joe would walk up to a house touching the gateposts, the window, door or wall, but if he was given a bit of food he would immediately take it and run away. Often he would walk down a road zig zagging from gate to gate, touching the posts as he passed. If a person met him in the streets he would more than likely touch his arm, shoulder or back with his finger.

Begging was his trade, and he called from house to house begging for food. His appetite was tremendous, and however large the leftovers were he would consume the lot in a very short time. Once he was given a massive bowl of potatoes and ate them with gusto and relish, but his enthusiasm got the better of him for he virtually choked himself to death. At the very last minute Joe was able to ask for a glass of water. He did not always meet with a favourable reception, as when he called on an elderly lady who did not like him and did not wish to give him any food. He hung around waiting but she was adamant. Finally, her patience wore out and she spoke angrily, *"Get out of the way; thou art as stupid as an ass! "*

Confused and tongue tied for a few moments, before running away, he replied, *"You are as stupid as two asses."*

Another time he was walking along the street very late at night when Mr. Jackson, a bookseller, met him. Since he was going home to have supper before going to bed, he asked Joe if he would like a snack. Naturally Joe was keen, and together they walked to Mr. Jackson's house. Inside Joe was made to sit at the kitchen table, while

Mr. Jackson went down into the cellar to get the bread and cheese. On his return he told Joe to eat as much as he liked, and with profound thanks Joe began cutting the bread and cheese. Shortly, Mr. Jackson could see Joe grimacing at the food.

When asked, Joe replied, *"This is funny cheese you gen me."*

"Is it, lad?" Mr. Jackson replied, picking up the cheese. Scrutinising it in his hand, he realised Joe had been eating soap!

Whenever there was a murder, jail break, rape or execution a special newspaper was printed giving the gruesome details. Joe had the job selling these, and this was when his true shyness became apparent. Instead of walking the streets shouting out loud about what the paper contained, he pushed them at people as they passed. He would say *"Gie me a ha'penny,"* but before they could take a copy and get their money out he had run away.

He did odd jobs for other people whenever they asked him. A Mr. Hallam asked Joe to wheel a barrow across a plank for him. Joe set off with the barrow, but about midway they parted company and fell into a ditch. Unhurt, he climbed back up to the plank. Mr. Hallam had seen Joe fall and was highly amused, and suggested to Joe that he purchase a couple of sheep eyes and fit them into the barrow. As it did not have eyes, how was he expected to wheel it across? With the eyes fixed on, Joe set off once more across the plank. Again, part way along he fell off, much to the merriment of Mr. Hallam. He laughed heartily, until suddenly he felt a cane smacked across his back. A Mr. Strutt who was passing by had seen the practical joke being played on Joe. Without a murmur from Mr. Hallam, Mr. Strutt told him never to tease the fellow again.

Joe was also teased by a gang called the Belper Nailers, but somehow he was able to withstand their teasing which was often of the cruelest form. This is all we know about this scatterbrained beggar. When he died in Belper workhouse no one claimed him and it was left to Derby, where he had been born, to administer the final rites .

Selected Bibliography

The Wanderings of Memory or Buxton of the Peak, A. G. Jewitt, 1815.

Derbyshire—Magna Britannia, Rev. Daniel Lyons, 1817.

The Peak Guide, S. Glover, 1830.

Three Centuries of Derbyshire Annals, Vols. I & 2, Rev. J. C. Cox, 1840.

The Life and Writings of Richard Furness, G. C. Holland, 1858.

Tales and Traditions of the High Peak, William Wood, 1862.

Derbyshire Gatherings, J. B. Robinson, 1866.

On Foot through the Peak, J. Croston, 1868.

Churches of Derbyshire, Vols. 1-4, Dr. J. C. Cox, 1875-9.

Bemrose's Guide to Derbyshire, 1878.

Punishments in the Olden Times, W. Andrews, 1881.

History of Derbyshire, J. Pendleton, 1886.

Bygone Derbyshire, W. Andrews, 1892.

Sheffield Miscellany, edited by J. J. Glassbay, 1897.

Haddon Hall, A. Charrington, 1900.

Peak Forest Register, edited by G. W. Marshall, 1901.

Romances of the Peak, W. Turner, 1901.

Haddon Hall, F. H. Cheetham, 1904.

Highways and Byeways in Derbyshire, J. B. Firth, 1905.

Haddon, the Manor, the Hall, its Lords and Traditions, G. Le Blanc Smith, 1906.

Plague Stricken Derbyshire Village of Eyam, Rev. J. M. J. Fletcher, 1909.

History of Stoney Middleton, T. E. Cowan, 1910.

Derbyshire, J. C. Cox, 1915.

A Sheaf of Essays by a Sheffield Antiquary, C. Drury, 1929.

Pinnacles of Peak History, C. Daniel, 1935.

Derbyshire, A. Mee, 1937.

Sheffield Clarion Ramblers' Handbook, 1940-1

A Peakland Portfolio, Clarence Daniel, 1948.

A History of Tideswell, W. Walker, 1951.

Derbyshire Miscellany, Vol. 2, No. 5, 1961.

An Illustrated Account of the Eyam Plague, C. Daniel, 1961.

Punishment in Derbyshire, John N. Merrill 1989.

Customs of the Peak District & Derbyshire, John N. Merrill 1989.

Derbyshire Folklore, John N. Merrill 1990.